Following Your Healing Path

A Bible Study and Companion Guide to
Linda Smith's Book *Called into Healing*

December, 2010

Blessings on your

healing path -

Linda Smith

Following Your Healing Path

A Bible Study and Companion Guide to
Linda Smith's Book *Called into Healing*

Rev. Tamara R. Dahlvang, M.Div.

Linda L. Smith, RN, MS, HTSM-CP/I
Director, Healing Touch Spiritual Ministry Program

HTSM Press
ARVADA, COLORADO

Following Your Healing Path
A Bible Study and Companion Guide to
Linda Smith's Book *"Called into Healing"*

A HTSM Press Book/January, 2011
All rights reserved.
Copyright © January, 2011 by Tamara Dahlvang and Linda Smith
Cover design by
Layout and Production by

***

No part of this book may be reproduced or transmitted in any form or by any means, electronic or mechanical, including photocopying, recording or by any information storage and retrieval system, without permission in writing from the publisher.

****

Scripture quotations are from the New Revised Standard Version of the Bible, copyright 1989 by the Division of Christian Education of the National Council of the Churches of Christ in the USA. Used by permission. All rights reserved.

****

Library of Congress Control Number: 2010935192

Dahlvang, Tamara R.; Smith, Linda L.
      Following Your Healing Path—
      A Bible Study and Companion Guide to Linda Smith's Book
      "Called into Healing"
   1. Spirituality 2. Prayer 3. Bible

ISBN 978-0-9765972-5-4

Published by HTSM Press
P.O. Box 741239, Arvada, Colorado 80006

9 8 7 6 5 4 3 2 1
Printed in the United States

DEDICATION

This book is dedicated to Christ, our healer. It is also dedicated to all who, through the ages, have brought the healing touch of Christ to others, especially the administrators, instructors, students and practitioners of the Healing Touch Spiritual Ministry Program.

Acknowledgments

Both of us have very busy lives, and many responsibilities. While we have labored in our writing, many people have encouraged us. Others have periodically stepped in to help us with our other responsibilities. Tammy's husband Jay and her sons James and Nate deserve thanks, as do Linda's staff—Pat, Mary and Darlene—who enabled her to do what she loves to do best—write and teach.

Table of Contents

Linda's Introduction

Almost a year ago, Tammy, a student in our advanced Healing Touch Spiritual Ministry program, approached me about developing a Companion Bible Study Guide to accompany my book *Called into Healing*. I thought it was an excellent idea—I had actually wanted to do such a guide but in the 10 years since first publishing *Called into Healing*, I had not found the time to do it. As an ordained minister, Tammy has the opportunity to often preach on the subject of healing. As you read her story in her introduction, I think you will agree with me that she is the perfect person to take up the leadership for this bible study guide based on the Gospel of Luke and written as a companion to my writing.

Luke's good news gospel is a favorite of mine. Luke, who tradition tells us was a physician and a traveling companion of Paul was obviously an educated man in the Hellenistic traditions, fluent in Greek, and possessed a keen sense of literary style. He authored two works—the third gospel and the Acts of the Apostles. These are companion books which continue to tell a great story of hero, prophet, liberator, miracle worker, martyr and divine being. We might call Luke a second generation follower of Jesus since it is doubtful whether he ever met Jesus personally. All the more reason to pay attention to the nuances of the stories found in his gospel. Luke had to have spent a great deal of time listening to, perhaps interviewing those eyewitnesses who knew Jesus first hand. I can imagine him tracking down the disciples and even those who were the recipients of Jesus' touch to gain their insights and feelings about this itinerant healer and preacher, cataloging their experiences and memories. Most probably he also had a copy of Mark's gospel and a book of sayings of Jesus which influenced his writing as well. Luke's audiences were clearly gentiles of Greek and Roman origin—people of culture and learning. Who was the Jesus that Luke portrays to this audience? Jesus is seen as a prophet, healer, savior, and as benefactor.

How are we using Luke's gospel stories in this bible study guide? The stories we have selected emphasize Jesus in his role as compassionate healer. Jesus was a role model for how we should treat one another. He was not a rabble rouser but healer of the highest vibration. Wherever he went, people loved to be in his presence, for power (energy) went out from him. We selected passages that in fact would be a companion guide to each of the chapters in my book *Called into Healing*. Although ten years have passed since I first wrote this book, students and readers alike have continued to draw comfort and support from what they find in its pages. *Called into Healing* is actually about all of our stories as we awaken to inner stirrings to reach out in healing ways to others.

As for my story in healing work, it's all in my book. I continue to teach and write about the work of Christianity which has a central focus of healing one another. My vision for healing to be the heart of a Christian life has not wavered but only grown stronger since I first began writing. By virtue of our baptism, we are called to heal one another, to be compassionate, loving presences who carry the Light of Christ into the world.

Tammy's Introduction

My first experience of Jesus' healing power took place at the altar of a small church in Northern California during a charismatic healing service. I don't remember much from that night, except for Jesus' name spoken, and the sense that I was loved beyond my ability to understand. When I went up to the altar at the front of the church, gentle hands were laid on me, prayers were voiced, and I felt the energy of a love I had never known. The preacher told Jesus' story, from Bethlehem to Golgotha, and the power of Christ for healing was there, available for me.

My eyes glazed over every time we went to church after that. Until one night in college, once again hurting, afraid and lonely, in a gray college lecture hall I heard the Bethlehem to Golgotha story. Again, Christ intervened in my life for mental and emotional healing. Again, I became a new person. Two years later I went to seminary to study the Bethlehem to Golgotha story in Greek. I earned a Masters of Divinity degree, and became an ordained Lutheran pastor. I cannot help but believe that my feet first slid into this path on that night when I was 6 years old and experienced the healing power of Christ. It was healing that led to my vocation.

Three years ago, during my first Healing Touch class, I experienced the power of Jesus to heal physical illness as well as mental and emotional ill-health. I had struggled with sciatica since the birth of my second son. This excruciating back pain was my excuse for getting the rest I needed, a valid reason to say no to many overwhelming demands that I felt obligated to meet. I sensed Jesus as I was receiving healing touch, and his loving energy once more embraced me. I felt like he stood in front of me, as he had once stood in front of the blind beggar and asked me "What do you want me to do for you? (Luke 18: 35-43). Just as the beggar made his livelihood from his illness, so I had begun to build part of my identity in begging pity from others.

Because I knew that story, I was able to put my own experience of

Christ's healing into the biblical perspective. It is my hope and prayer that this Bible Study will help you do likewise. It is a complicated fact that in Christ's grace healing is not automatic. We hold onto pain and illnesses for many reasons. I knew that Jesus wouldn't judge me if I wanted to hold onto my pain. It was my choice to make. I also knew that if I wanted him to, he both could and would heal me as I was receiving healing touch. Like the blind beggar I chose to ask him for healing, and he did heal me. Through human hands, he touched me. The pain traveled along my sciatic nerve and left my body.

Healing Touch is practiced by Christians and non-Christians. For me, Healing Touch is an experience of the love that I identify with being filled with the Spirit of Christ. It is a manifestation of that reality that Jesus called "The Kingdom of God." The love Christ embodied, the suffering he endured for the sake of his Kingdom, the healing he brought to others, his triumph over death … this Bethlehem to Golgotha story we discover within the pages of scripture is the story of God's revelation of love that heals beyond our ken.

But I feel Christians have lost Christ's story. The week after I finished my first Healing Touch class, a beloved parishioner phoned me to tell me about the terrible pain he felt in his knees. This pain kept him from sleeping, and nothing he took for it helped him. I told him about Healing Touch, and asked him if I could give him a treatment. This offer was met with grim silence. "Healing," he said finally. "I went to a healing service in a church once. Didn't do any good. No, thank you, I just don't believe in it."

This man was a cradle Christian, and he didn't believe in healing. Was he reading the same Bible I was? How was this possible that he didn't believe in healing? Jesus preached, taught, exorcised demons and healed people. He sent his disciples out to do likewise. Did he think Jesus had changed? I didn't know what to say as I felt tears well up in my throat. Christ Jesus is a healer … and this dear Christian man does not believe it, despite biblical sermons. How can he ever know how good Jesus is if he doesn't believe in healing? Perhaps he sees his knee pain as his cross … maybe he doesn't want to get his hopes up … but why refuse even to ask Christ for healing? I did not, and do not, understand it. It seemed to me akin to refusing to breathe because he didn't believe in oxygen.

It is because there are so many people like my dear parishioner who do not believe in healing that Linda and I saw the need for this Bible study. This study is to encourage you who give Healing Touch within the church, so that you don't get discouraged when you encounter similar attitudes. You are carrying on the biblical story. You are the disciples sent to usher in God's kingdom. Please, don't ever forget that. Christ's love, which is a manifestation of the Holy Spirit present among us, flows through our hands into others, blessing both the givers and the recipients of this love.

So read the Bible, sisters and brothers in Christ. In the words of Eugene Peterson, "eat this book." Discover Christ within its pages, and you will discover personal healing and a commission to work for Christ for the healing of the world.

How To Use This Bible Study and Companion Guide

Following your Healing Path—A Bible Study and Companion Guide to Linda Smith's Book "Called into Healing" was written for Christian students and practitioners of Healing Touch created by Janet Mentgen in the 1980s and Healing Touch Spiritual Ministry developed by Linda Smith ten years later. It is our hope that this guide will help your faith to inform your experience of giving and receiving a healing touch. It is also our hope that it will provide room for your experience of this healing work to illumine your faith in a new way.

Luke's gospel contains many stories of healing. Jesus' healing ministry was central to his proclamation that good news is here; the people whose minds and bodies he healed were visible evidence of what Jesus called "the Kingdom of God." We have used some of these healing incidents to parallel the messages contained in the 9 chapters in Linda Smith's book *Called into Healing, Reclaiming Our Judeo-Christian Legacy of Healing Touch*. Each session will consider a passage from Luke and a chapter from *Called into Healing*. Our purpose is not so much to explain further what is in *Called into Healing* as it is to draw parallels and new insights from the scriptures and our life experiences.

This study guide can be used in study groups or used alone in one's own reflective meditation. Each session begins with a Gathering—a getting acquainted time of sharing, followed by the Healing Word from Luke's Gospel. There will be thought questions for discussion or reflection. Following this will be selected Passages from *Called into Healing*, paralleling Luke's message.

Each session will then have reflections and or exercises on Healing Others and Healing Ourselves. Some sessions will have meditations while others will have steps from various healing techniques which can be practiced on others. All of the meditations and healing techniques have been contributed by Linda Smith and come from the courses in the Healing Touch Spiritual Ministry program.

We hope that this coupling of Luke's Gospel and *Called into Healing* will be inspiring for you in your call to healing ministry for others. Isaiah wrote about the voice he heard calling to him "whom shall I send?" We encourage you to listen to that voice as it calls to you to help restore healing in Christianity.

Note to the Reader

We want to clarify our use of the words "healing touch" used throughout this biblical guide. When we capitalize these words we are specifically referring to the educational program developed by Janet Mentgen promoted worldwide today by the Healing Touch Program under the capable leadership of Janet's daughter, Lisa Mentgen Gordon and directed by Cynthia Hutchinson RN, DNsc, HTCP, HTCI. When we use the lower case for healing touch, we are using the words in a generic sense, referring to both the healing work of Healing Touch (HT) and Healing Touch Spiritual Ministry (HTSM). HTSM grew out of Healing Touch as a separate educational program taught from a Judeo-Christian perspective specifically for those who desire to restore healing in Christian churches and institutions. The Healing Touch Spiritual Ministry approach is based in the scriptures and integrates prayer, energy healing and anointing with healing oils. In the letter of James, Chapter 5 verse 14, it asks the question: "are any among you sick?" "Then they are to call in the elders who must pray, [lay-on hands] and anoint them with oil in the name of the Lord." The aim of this program is to restore and remind us of our Christian duty to heal one another with a healing touch.

Conflict between Christ and His Culture

Luke 4:16-30
Called into Healing, chapter 1

Gathering

Once everyone has arrived, pass out name tags. Ask everyone to write their name on their name tag and to put it on. Invite everyone to introduce him or herself. If people already know each other well, you can skip lengthy introductions.

Ask everyone how they first learned about the work of Healing Touch or Healing Touch Spiritual Ministry. When did they take their first course? What was it that drew them to this healing work? Has giving and receiving healing touch affected their understanding of God? What do they hope to learn from studying "Following Your Healing Path?"

Healing Word

After he was baptized and tempted in the wilderness, Jesus began to teach people in synagogues throughout Galilee. People were impressed by the authority with which he spoke and so he developed a reputation as an amazing teacher. When he went home to Nazareth for the first time after his ministry had begun, he went to the synagogue he had once worshiped in as a boy. He was invited to address his old friends and neighbors. The words he read from Isaiah are frequently referred to as Christ's "inaugural address."

The Rejection of Jesus at Nazareth

"When he came to Nazareth, where he had been brought up, he went to the synagogue on the Sabbath day, as was his custom. He stood up to read, and the scroll of the prophet Isaiah was given to him. He unrolled the scroll and found the place where it was written:

> *'The Spirit of the Lord is upon me,*
> *because he has anointed me to bring good news to the poor.*
> *He has sent me to proclaim release to the captives*
> *and recovery of sight to the blind,*
> *to let the oppressed go free, to proclaim the year of the*
>   *Lord's favor.'*

And he rolled up the scroll, gave it back to the attendant, and sat down. The eyes of all in the synagogue were fixed on him. Then he began to say to them, 'Today this scripture has been fulfilled in your hearing.' All spoke well of him and were amazed at the gracious words that came from his mouth. They said, 'Is not this Joseph's son?'

He said to them, 'Doubtless you will quote to me this proverb, "Doctor, cure yourself!" And you will say, "Do here also in your home town the things that we have heard you did at Capernaum."' And he said, 'Truly I tell you, no prophet is accepted in the prophet's home town. But the truth is, there were many widows in Israel in the time of Elijah, when the heaven was shut up for three years and six months, and there was a severe famine over all the land; yet Elijah was sent to none of them except to a widow at Zarephath in Sidon. There were also many lepers in Israel in the time of the prophet Elisha, and none of them was cleansed except Naaman the Syrian.'

When they heard this, all in the synagogue were filled with rage. They got up, drove him out of the town, and led him to the brow of the hill on which their town was built, so that they might hurl him off the cliff. But he passed through the midst of them and went on his way." Luke 4: 16-30

The contrast between Jesus' reception in his hometown of Nazareth and his earlier reception in synagogues full of strangers is painful. Why did people who didn't know him welcome him with glad amazement, while those who knew him well were offended? When Mark tells a similar story in his gospel, he adds this poignant fact:

> "And he {Jesus} could do no deed of power there, except that he laid his hands on a few sick people and cured them. And he was amazed at their unbelief". Mark 6:5-6

It is not only Jesus' intention to heal people that matters: they must also be open to receiving his help. Doubt … the deep-rooted refusal to believe that Jesus has power … blocks Jesus' power. The energy of Jesus, the fire of the Holy Spirit, will not permeate the barrier that someone's deliberate refusal to be open to him sets up.

Historically, Jesus reminded them, the people who were most open to the power of God weren't always the ones we'd expect. During the time of Elijah, when the famine was severe, God did not send Elijah to a Hebrew widow. He sent him to a widow from Zaraphath in Sidon—a Gentile, an outsider. Presumably this wasn't because God didn't want to save an Israelite widow. It was because God had to use someone who was open to the miracle that was about to unfold. It took faith for the widow of Zarapheth to use the last of her flour and oil to make bread for the prophet, instead of saving it for herself and her son. She was open to the promise Elijah made to her when he told her that she and her son would not starve if she fed him first. She believed that it was possible that God might miraculously intervene to feed her family.

But skepticism doesn't always bar the Spirit's way. When Elisha told the Syrian army general Naaman that God would heal him of his leprosy if he bathed in the river Jordan seven times, Naaman was incredulous. He was ready to go home. But on second thought he listened to his advisers when they pointed out that bathing seven times in the river was such a small thing to do that it was foolish not to do it when the payoff might be so great. He was open, however remotely, to the possibility that God might heal him—and God did. Naaman emerged from the water with skin like a young boy's. Openness and some skepticism may coexist. But what Jesus encountered in Nazareth was more than skepticism. It was disbelief, mixed with growing hostility.

The disbelief faced by Jesus in Nazareth was matched only by the disbelief he faced among leaders of his own religious community. Again and again, they challenged Jesus. As Chapter 1 of *Called into Healing* describes, there were prescribed procedures for healing. After someone became ill, they were to pray to God, to search their heart and repent, then to offer a sacrifice. Only after these steps were completed were they to seek help from a physician. When Jesus healed people, the religious traditions surrounding healing were side-stepped—illness (the consequence of sin) was removed without prayer, repentance or sacrifice. People simply approached Jesus and asked him for mercy. Healing happened because he touched them and they were made well. If illness was caused by sin, then Jesus negated the consequences of sin when he healed the sick with a touch. For a rabbi to touch or to eat with sinners prior to repentance, ritual sacrificial, and restoration to the community, was unclean—even repulsive. So their hearts were closed to him. They felt, down deep in their bones, that Jesus' ministry was not faithful to the God they worshiped. Like the Nazarenes, they put up a wall of disbelief that rebuffed his ministry. This wall rendered him powerless to help them.

Questions for Discussion

1. Have you found that people who are religious are more likely to be open or closed to healing ministry? Why do you think that is?

2. Have you ever questioned why some faithful Christians remain ill despite prayers for healing while people who don't seem religious at all recover? Is God playing "favorites?"

3. Do you believe people bring on their own illnesses through behaviors like addictions, greed, selfishness, and other harmful practices?

4. Has your healing work given you new sight (or insight), freed you from oppression, and been a way for you to proclaim God's favor to others?

5. What kinds of things can we do to raise our awareness of Jesus' power in our own lives? How can we be more open to what he gives us?

Called into Healing, chapter 1 (pp.4-17)

The ancient Hebrews struck a bargain with God in the form of the covenant. This bond tied them to Yahweh, the source of all that is. Yahweh, in turn, agreed to care for the chosen ones. Obedience of the nation and physical health were linked, just as disobedience and disease were linked ... p.5

1. How would the belief that God would care for obedient people have affected the way the Hebrew people viewed the sick?

2. When he spoke to the people in Nazareth, Jesus reminded them that in the past God had healed outsiders, people who were not part of the covenant. Given their covenant theology, why would this reminder have been so challenging (and offensive) to them?

The most positive reference to the roles of the physician and medicine is in the Apocryphal book of Ecclesiasticus (Sirach). This passage describes the conditions under which God will heal. Notice in this passage that in order to be made well or "whole" there are four things required:
   1. Pray first to the Lord for deliverance
   2. Look within and see where you have missed the mark, then repent
   3. Make an offering, the best you have
   4. Finally, submit to the physician ... p.10

3. In what order do we pray, repent, sacrifice and submit to the physician today?

4. After they become sick, some people place great hope in changing their lifestyles or in renewing their religious practices. How is this similar to looking within to see where we have missed the mark? How is it different?

5. What do you think the phrase "medicines of the earth" is referring to? Something people made or something God made?

On pages 14-17 of *Called into Healing*, Smith describes the beginning of Jesus' ministry, and the challenges he posed to the understanding of illness and healing that was common in his culture.

6. What cultural understandings of illness and healing does Jesus challenge in us today?

7. Why do many people today believe healing should best left to the "professionals?"

Smith writes that—

Connecting with God, he {Jesus} was able to release the fire and energy of God in the form of healing … he employed different healing methods … he healed through his very presence, through love, word, touch, faith … p.16

8. How is Christ present when you do healing touch work?

9. Jesus encouraged the people with words of hope. How does healing touch restore hope?

10. Jesus healed through the power of God and he empowered his followers to heal as he did. How has Jesus empowered you to give a healing touch?

Healing Others: Being a Healing Presence for Others

Jesus' only marked failure to heal and work miracles was among the people he already knew. They couldn't accept that someone they had known for so long could do the things they had heard he could do.

Their expectations that he was powerless closed their hearts to the power of his loving intention.

Most people who give Healing Touch have encountered the attitude that it is somehow quackery or witchcraft. This attitude can even be held by those who love us, and whom we love. It's very hard when we know that someone would benefit from receiving healing touch, but they are not open. Perhaps the best way to help others in this case is to simply be a healing presence for them.

On page 137 of *Called into Healing,* Smith lists some of the qualities of a healing presence. It may be helpful to read through her list of qualities, and to consciously adopt one or more of them toward people who are not open to healing at this time. This will not only help them, but it will help you to counteract any feelings of frustration or impatience with them. Perhaps the healing that your presence brings to them will help them to arrive at a place where they will be more open to receiving healing.

Healing Ourselves: At the Pool of Bethesda[1]

When Jesus went home to Nazareth, he went home to his past. Often, when we gaze on our pasts, there is some pain there. We have all made mistakes … and we have all been hurt by the people who know (and perhaps love) us best. Likewise, we have probably hurt others.

You can use this meditation to come to peace with events from your past that are holding you back, or shutting you down. You can also use it to request further openness to faith in Christ's power to heal. Enjoy this beautiful meditation, and may it bring you healing and peace.

> After you have become quiet within, read the story from John about the healing at the pool of Bethesda. Have your journal nearby for reflection.

---

1. Linda Smith, *Healing Touch Spiritual Ministry 104 Student Notebook* (Arvada, Colorado: HTSM Press, 2010), pp. 67-68. Inspiration for this meditation comes from Thomas Droege, *The Healing Presence,* pp. 34-37.

St. John tells us the story of a man who had been ill for many years who was at the pool at Bethesda.

"Now in Jerusalem by the Sheep Gate there is a pool, called in Hebrew Bethesda, which has five porticoes. In these lay many invalids—blind, lame, and paralyzed. One man was there who had been ill for thirty-eight years. When Jesus saw him lying there and knew that he had been there a long time, he said to him, 'Do you want to be made well?' The sick man answered him, 'Sir, I have no one to put me into the pool when the water is stirred up; and while I am making my way, someone else steps down ahead of me.' Jesus said to him, 'Stand up, take your mat and walk.' At once the man was made well, and he took up his mat and began to walk." John 5:2-9

- Begin to relax your body, gently closing your eyes. Feel your body against the chair and comfortably settle down. Allow your breath to bring you to a stillness within. *(pause)*

- Water is a powerful symbol for purification, healing, power and life. The waters of baptism are an expression of life-giving power for Christians. In your mind now, bring yourself to the healing waters of the pool at Bethesda. *(pause)*

- Everyone knows that from time to time an angel of the Lord descends and stirs the waters and whoever enters the water afterward, experiences healing in body, mind and spirit. *(pause)*

- Imagine that you have just arrived at this beautiful pool, notice the colors, feel the delightful breeze. There are many others who also have heard about these famous waters and are crowding around the edges. In fact there is no space for you near the water—so you find a place to rest further away where you can still see the water. *(pause)*

- Now that you have a place, begin to reflect on why you would want to enter these healing waters. What within you is in need of healing? Is it your body? Your mind? Your emotions? Or, perhaps it is your spirit that cries out for God's healing. *(pause)*

- As you reflect on your own need of healing, you notice the faces and the bodies of those around you who also look for healing. Some appear in greater need than you—some are young, some old—some are more agile than you and able to get to the waters ahead of you. *(pause)*

- As you reflect, imagine that you see Jesus approaching. He walks past all the others and comes directly to you, sitting down beside you. Looking directly into your eyes, he asks,

- "Do you want to be healed?" Take some time answering. This is a very important question. Sometimes we hold on to our lack of wholeness for various reasons. Check inside. Are you holding onto something that keeps you in dis-harmony? Something that keeps you in pain physically, emotionally, or spiritually? Tell Jesus about any reluctance you might have about being healed. *(pause)*

- Now imagine Jesus taking you by the hand and leading you to the pool. What does he do? What does he say about the water? Allow the story to unfold before you. How do you respond? You may quietly reflect or journal your dialogue and what happens with Jesus.

Jesus: Physician of Forgiveness

Luke 5: 17-26
Called into Healing, chapter 2

Gathering

As everyone arrives, give them slips of paper. On the paper, ask them to write: "Forgiveness means … " Ask them to fill in the blank. Once everyone is done, go around the group, with everyone sharing their response.

Ask the group to reflect on an occasion when they have felt unforgiven. What did feeling unforgiven do to them physically, mentally and spiritually? How does feeling unforgiven effect your energy?

Now take a minute to think about a time when you have withheld forgiveness because someone has hurt you. What did feeling unforgiving do to you physically, mentally and spiritually? How did withholding forgiveness affect your energy?

Unforgiveness can make us physically ill. We are freed from its prison by the promises God has made to us in baptism. If it feels appropriate, you can take some time as a group to remember your baptisms. Dipping your fingers in a small bowl of water, you can draw the sign of the cross on the forehead of the person closest to you and say "_____(name), child of God, you have been sealed by the Holy Spirit and marked with the cross of Christ forever. Walk in the light, as a forgiven and a forgiving child of God." Then the person who has just been marked by the cross can take the bowl of water, and seal the person sitting by them … and so on, until everyone has been sealed and marked. Then you can join hands together and say the Lord's

Prayer, paying special attention to "forgive our sins as we forgive those who sin against us."

Healing Word

In many of the healing accounts in the gospels, Jesus healed people without telling them that their sins were forgiven. But there were times—the woman who was caught in adultery in John 8 and the woman who was publicly identified as a sinner Luke 7—when Jesus actually told them "your sins are forgiven."

Notice that even though he was clearly in need of physical healing, Jesus forgave the paralyzed man before he healed him physically. Our need for forgiveness can be more urgent than our physical illnesses, although it may also be much less obvious.

The Healing of the Paralytic

"One day, while he was teaching, Pharisees and teachers of the law were sitting nearby (they had come from every village of Galilee and Judea and from Jerusalem); and the power of the Lord was with him to heal. Just then some men came, carrying a paralyzed man on a bed. They were trying to bring him in and lay him before Jesus; but finding no way to bring him in because of the crowd, they went up on the roof and let him down with his bed through the tiles into the middle of the crowd in front of Jesus. When he saw their faith, he said, 'Friend, your sins are forgiven you.'

Then the scribes and the Pharisees began to question, 'Who is this who is speaking blasphemies? Who can forgive sins but God alone?' When Jesus perceived their questionings, he answered them, 'Why do you raise such questions in your hearts? Which is easier, to say, "Your sins are forgiven you", or to say, "Stand up and walk"? But so that you may know that the Son of Man has authority on earth to forgive sins'—he said to the one who was paralyzed—'I say to you, stand up and take your bed and go to your home.'

Immediately he stood up before them, took what he had been lying on, and went to his home, glorifying God. Amazement seized all of them, and they glorified God and were filled with awe, saying, 'We have seen strange things today.'" (Luke 5:17-26, NRSV)

When she was in her twenties, Sally suffered what was later diagnosed as a "psychotic break from reality." Her son Max was very young at the time. She received treatment three years after the onset of her mental illness, but during those years Max was terribly abused by his alcoholic step-father. Sally never forgave herself for her failure to protect her child. Intuitive Max picked up on her guilt. As a teenager he blamed her for everything that went wrong in his life. In adolescence, he told Sally that he would never forgive her. Sally became clinically depressed overnight.

Both Sally and Max were crippled by haunting memories of the past until, over a decade later, Max himself received healing. Part of Max's healing was his own repentance. His bitterness and resentment had kept his fragile mother, who more than anything else yearned for his love, in bondage to his anger for years. He had abused her as cruelly as his step-father had abused him. His attachment to the power of victimhood had to be broken before his mother could heal.

We are all connected in a web of emotional attachments, and because Sally would not break her attachment to her desire for her son to love her, she could only recover after he forgave her. Refusing to forgive another person is the ultimate power-play. Feeling unforgiven is toxic. When we know that we have hurt someone who cannot or will not let the pain go, who may even regularly relive it, we may feel forced to relive it with them. Unforgiveness, whether we're the ones who need to be forgiven or the ones who need to forgive someone else, locks us into the prison of the space and time when the incident(s) for which we need forgiveness happened. Grace frees us. Unforgiveness creates an energy cord between two people that is filled with resentment. Grace turns those cords into conduits of love.

It was still early in Jesus' ministry when he forgave the paralytic, and then cured him. The healing happened in a house filled with onlookers, including religious leaders from every village in Galilee, and Judea. That there were clergy from Jerusalem who had come to see Jesus is important. Jerusalem was the center of Jewish religious life. If Jerusalem was paying attention to him, Jesus' ministry was renowned.

Jesus read everyone's heart when he healed the paralytic. First, he saw the faith deep within the man and his friends. When he saw their faith, he told the man "Friend, your sins are forgiven you." That Jesus would forgive someone their sins doesn't surprise us, but for the scribes and the Pharisees it was incomprehensible. Only God had the keys to free people from their past sins. Who did Jesus think he was?

> *"Which is easier, to say 'Your sins are forgiven you,' or to say 'Stand up and walk?' But so that you may know that the Son of Man has authority on earth to forgive sins"*—he said to the paralytic—*"I say to you, take up your bed and go to your home."* Mark 2:8b-11.
> The man did.

The man's mental and spiritual healing were connected to his physical healing. Both paralyzed him. After this healing, the religious leaders began what was to become a constant nagging refrain of complaints: Jesus ate with tax collectors and sinners … he healed on the Sabbath … he blasphemed by claiming to be able to forgive sins. He responded that those who were well had no need of a physician, but the sick did need one. He had not come for the righteous, those who saw within themselves no need to repent. He had come to call sinners to repentance (Luke 5:31-32). And there we have it—Jesus is the physician whose diagnosis is often sin, and whose remedy for sin is forgiveness.

Those locked in the prison of unforgiveness are rarely without physical suffering as well. Often, like the paralytic, they are in search of physical healing. Joyfully, Jesus delights to heal and to forgive. In time, the spiritual healing of forgiveness to remedy sin came to be understood as the primary goal of Jesus' ministry. Physical healing was allowed to fall by the wayside as the church developed into an institution. While they functioned beautifully in tandem when Jesus forgave and healed the paralytic, over time physical healing and forgiveness became separated.

Jesus both healed and forgave freely. Jesus loved to heal. It was his passion. He healed people wherever he went *(Called into Healing,* pp.203-204). He healed people on the Sabbath, which filled the religious leaders with rage (Luke 6:11). His early followers healed with the same regularity *(Called,* p.205). The physical healing was sometimes meant to be the tangible sign of the intangible reality of forgiveness. But not always. Throughout the gospels, we read that Jesus' heart was constantly moved by compassion for the sick. He usually healed people because he was moved by pity.

He is still here among us, and his love for people has not lessened. The reticence of the church to proclaim that Christ can and does heal and to engage wholeheartedly in healing ministries, is not justified by the biblical witness.

Questions for Discussion

1. Have you ever known someone whose friends have supported them like the friends of the paralytic did? What does it mean today to "raise the roof" in prayer for someone?

2. Do you think that most people who hope for physical healing are also hoping for spiritual/ mental and emotional healing?

3. The man was physically paralyzed. How can feeling like we have done something terrible, and that God will not forgive us, paralyze us? Do you think that our physical illnesses ever mirror or mimic our spiritual reality?

4. How do you understand the link between forgiveness and healing?

5. Jesus said *"Be perfect as your heavenly Father is perfect,"* (Matthew 5:48). That means that God is all love. When we return to the Father asking forgiveness, we are restored the perfection God created. Is this not what is meant by healing?

Called into Healing, Chapter 2 (pp. 29-57)

We begin to see in those first 200 years of the Christian
experience differences of opinion develop about the role of
healing among Christians. Some saw healing as natural Christian
behavior, while others thought that it was only to be used to prove
to heretics that Jesus was God ... Decision-making for the whole
community was set down in a patriarchal fashion that mirrored
their patriarchal society. (p31)

1. What differences of opinion about the role of healing in the
   church have you encountered? Can you see the reasoning behind
   more than one perspective, or is the role of healing in the church
   a cut-and-dried issue for you?

2. Smith describes how the influx of nominal Christians affected
   the culture of the church, resulting in healing becoming
   relegated to the sacraments, and to formal liturgical healing
   services. Healing went from being part of everyday Christian life
   to being confined to the church and controlled by the clergy.
   How can we reclaim our healing tradition?

Augustine taught that God sent affliction not so much as
punishment—as the Jewish people believed—but rather to purify
the souls of men and women. Physical suffering was accepted as
necessary to the attainment of spiritual perfection. This is
substantiated in many New Testament writings (p.32).

3. Jesus said that the reason that a man had been born blind was so
   that his healing would reveal God's works (John 9:3). How can it
   be true that the blind man's healing reveals God's works, and
   also true that illness can sometimes bring us closer to God?

4. If you believe that God is the essence of pure love, how can God
   also be the one who punishes and sends affliction? This is not a
   New Testament belief but is of the Old Testament.

5. Aquinas emphasized that the soul is more important than the body (*Called*, p.43). Do you believe that the body and soul can be viewed as separate?

6. Do you think it was inevitable that the separation between body and soul would lead to what Smith calls "the medical model" (*Called*, p.47)?

7. In history we seem to have forgotten the wisdom of treating the body, mind, and spirit as an integrated whole. How can this be restored today in healthcare and in spiritual care?

There is much to learn from other cultures and other spiritual paths, but in the end Christians will weigh this knowledge with what Jesus taught... We can look to the scriptures themselves, to Christian mysticism, to our understanding of the gifts of the Holy Spirit, and to the saints and holy ones who have gone before us (p.56).

8. Have you had a hard time putting the eastern language and concepts used to teach Healing Touch into a Christian context? What has helped you?

9. How is healing viewed in your church? Smith speaks of a biblical mandate to teach, preach and heal (p.57). To what extent is that mandate a present reality in your congregation or religious community?

For the Healing of Others: Assessing the Unseen

Smith advises that the first step in an assessment is to **ask** the person what they would like to have you do. If Jesus had asked that question of the paralytic and his friends, the answer might have been the obvious one—the man wanted to be able to walk.

Since Christ's intention for healing may be different from the person's request, Smith also advises that we **observe** the person, asking

God for guidance in seeing the areas that need help. Following observation, she says to **listen inside**.

> "An intuitive sense may come to you as you connect with the wisdom within your heart ... pray for clarity" (p.103.)

A good assessment will lead you to know, with an inner knowing, what to do next (p.104.) It is Christ who is healing through us, using our hands to meet the person's deepest need (which may be physical or spiritual or both).

Healing Ourselves:
On Bringing a Friend or Loved One to Jesus

Who do you love so much that you would tear off the roof of a house to bring them to Jesus? It may seem strange to put a meditation for distant healing under the "Healing Ourselves" heading, but anyone who has urgently sought healing for someone else knows that to see a loved one healed is to be healed ourselves. This is an exercise in Distant Healing which brings both our loved ones and ourselves before Christ.

On Bringing a Friend or Loved One to Jesus[2]

> This guided exercise is a meditative form of healing prayer for a friend or loved one who is in need of healing in body, mind or spirit. The scriptures encourage us to pray for one another and we are told to ask for what we need. First, prayerfully read these Scriptural passages about healing.

> *"They brought to him a demoniac who was blind and mute; and he cured him, so that the one who had been mute could speak and see."* Matt. 12:22

---

2. Linda Smith, *Healing Touch Spiritual Ministry 104 Student Notebook, "Forming a Healing Practice,"* Arvada, Colorado, HTSM Press, 2009, p. 77.

"Just then a Canaanite woman from that region came out and started shouting, 'Have mercy on me, Lord, Son of David; my daughter is tormented by a demon.'... 'Woman, great is your faith! Let it be done for you as you wish. And her daughter was healed instantly." Matt. 15:22, 28.

"Lord, have mercy on my son, for he is an epileptic and he suffers terribly; he often falls into the fire and often into the water ... And Jesus rebuked the demon, and it came out of him and the boy was cured instantly." Matt.17:15, 18.

"Now Simon's mother-in-law was in bed with a fever, and they told him about her at once. He came and took her by the hand and lifted her up. Then the fever left her, and she began to serve them." Mark 1:30-31.

"Then some people came, bringing to him a paralyzed man, carried by four of them ... When Jesus saw their faith, he said to the paralytic, 'Son your sins are forgiven.'" Mark 2:3, 5

"Some brought a blind man to him and begged him to touch him." Mark 8:22

"People were bringing little children to him in order that he might touch them." Mark 10:13

- Come into a quiet place within and allow your breath to slow you down. Breathe in now the breath of God and feel that healing light spread throughout your entire being—body, mind, and spirit.

- Ask the Holy Spirit to show you the one who most needs your prayers at this moment—a friend or loved one—someone you know personally. (pause) This person may need healing of spirit, emotions, or body. You may not even know the full depth of their brokenness. Wait and see who comes to mind. *(pause)*

- Imagine that you are walking with this friend or loved one along a road. Up ahead, you notice a crowd has gathered and they are quietly listening to a teacher. As you draw closer, you recognize the teacher as none other than Jesus himself. *(pause)*

- You bring your loved one to the group which makes room for both of you. After speaking with a number of other people in the group, Jesus turns his attention to you and recognizes you in his greeting. You tell him about your loved one who you have brought with you and about their needs as you perceive them. Jesus listens intently and you sense compassion flowing from his heart and his eyes. *(pause)*

- Then, Jesus turns his attention to your loved one. For the next few moments, watch and see what Jesus says and does with your friend. *(long pause)*

- As you prepare to leave your friend/loved one with Jesus, ask Jesus what you are to be doing to help your friend/loved one. Hear what Jesus tells you. (pause) Now, continue on your journey along the road knowing in your heart that your friend/loved one is in the care of Jesus.

- When you are ready, quietly return to this place. Again, allow your breath to help you come back to the present moment.

SESSION 3

Touch That Heals

Luke 5: 12-14, 27-32
Called into Healing, chapter 3

Gathering

Once everyone arrives, invite them to hold out their hands. Ask them to name three people they've touched in the past week. Why do we touch people? What does touch convey that words don't? If there is time, ask the group to join hands. Everyone can hold hands, with their left hands receiving (palm up) and their right hands giving energy (palm down). As the energy is passed from person to person, invite people to think a loving thought about the person on their right.

Healing Word

In Jesus' day, there were very strict prohibitions surrounding touch. Women were to be touched only by other women, or by male members of their family. No woman was to be touched when she was menstruating. Lepers were never to be touched. People who were living in a state of constant and public sin were not to be touched, nor even socialized with, by religious people. If a righteous person did touch someone who was unclean, then they became unclean themselves. In his short ministry, Jesus broke each and every one of these rules not because he was a rebel and a rule breaker, but because he saw unnecessary suffering and knew he could do something about it. When he touched those who were suffering, healing flowed out of him. Healing and touch were frequently entwined.

The Leper

"Once, when he was in one of the cities, there was a man covered with leprosy. When he saw Jesus, he bowed with his face to the ground and begged him, 'Lord, if you choose, you can make me clean.' Then Jesus stretched out his hand, touched him, and said, 'I do choose. Be made clean.' Immediately the leprosy left him. And he ordered him to tell no one. 'Go', he said, 'and show yourself to the priest, and, as Moses commanded, make an offering for your cleansing, for a testimony to them.'" Luke 5: 12-14

He was covered with leprosy. He was supposed to wear tattered clothes, to cover his mouth in the presence of others, and to shout "Unclean, unclean!" wherever he went, so that everyone would know to keep their distance. He lived in a segregated area, with the other lepers. No one was allowed to touch him, not even members of his own family. No one was even allowed to touch anything he had touched.

He asked to be made clean—he never asked Jesus to touch him. And Jesus, who used a variety of healing techniques, could have healed him without touch. Without hesitation, he stretched out his hand and touched the leper. Technically, touching the leper before he had shown himself to the priest and had been declared clean should have made Jesus unclean. So should eating with tax collectors and sinners, or touching the menstruating woman and the dead little girl. When Jesus touched people, the opposite of what should have happened— happened. Instead of contagion spreading to Jesus, health spread to the person he was healing.

Today, many are still concerned that germs will contaminate a healthy person when the healthy person touches the sick one. Common sense would dictate that we take sensible precautions when we're working with someone who is infectious. That said, a fundamental premise of healing touch work is that someone with centered, loving energy, who is holding the intention to help another, will have a beneficial effect on the health of the person with whom they are working. It's the opposite of what Linda Smith calls "the germ

model." Illness may be contagious … but health is contagious, too!
The Spirit of Jesus is contagious. His healing power is contagious
within us when we reach out to others with the intention to be
channels of his continued healing. Blessedly, being used by the Spirit of
Christ to channel this energy has a profound healing effect on the
healer as well.

Touch today is not without controversy either. A member of a
church with a Healing Touch Spiritual Ministry waited until the line to
shake the pastor's hand had dwindled before he approached her. "I
want to know what goes on in that room with that bed (massage table)
in there," he said. "I want to know why we can't just pray for people
like we always have. Why do they have to lie down? Why do they have
to be touched all over?" His wife, who stood next to him, murmured
"There just shouldn't be a bed in a church. It's not good." This is a true
story. A massage table is actually more comfortable than asking
someone to lie down on the floor or on a hard conference table.

What could the pastor say? The answer to his question is "We don't
know why God has chosen this means, but God has." And his question
begged a responding one: "How can you stand in the way of Christ's
healing? How can you allow your own issues with touch to threaten
this healing ministry, to curtail God's kingdom to fit your
expectations?"

People today are in bondage to their taboos surrounding touch just
as they were in Jesus' day. Love itself can be rejected when it doesn't fit
into our notions of how things should be. There are good reasons for
approaching touch carefully. There are even better ones for breaking
some societal taboos (such as lying down to receive healing touch in
church). It's important to heed Zach Thomas' words of caution, as he
points out that touch can and has been used to abuse and misuse others
(*Called into Healing*, p.61). But churches that have set up their Healing
Touch ministries using ISHA's *Suggested Guidelines and Policies*[3] will be
safe places for touch. Perhaps a good metaphor for touch is fire. When

---

3. Linda Smith, *Suggested Guidelines and Policies for a Healing Ministry*, 5th edition, Arvada,
   Colorado: HTSM Press, April, 2010.

fire is out of control, it is destructive. If we had never harnessed fire though, there would be no civilization as we know it.

Given the close connection between our bodies and our psyches, it is true that inappropriate touch can do incalculable harm. Given that same close connection, it is just as true that loving touch can heal. It is also true that we may be viewed with the same suspicion and mistrust with which Jesus was viewed when we break societal taboos surrounding touch.

Questions for Discussion

1. Who in today's society do we consider "unclean?" Do we hesitate to touch them? If so, is it because we see them as "contagious" in some way or among the "untouchables of society?"

2. Today, who are people allowed to touch, and who are we not allowed to touch? Why?

3. Are there people to whom you wouldn't want to give healing touch because it would make you uncomfortable?

4. I have noticed that when I experience love for others, I seem to experience greater health myself. The converse is true as well (disliking someone seems to negatively influence my health). Thich Nhat Hanh explores this notion in some of his works as well, inviting us to think of someone we love before we begin meditating. How does loving others affect your health?

5. When I am able to remember my love for my family, it profoundly affects them. They appear to flourish and blossom. How does your love for them affect your family's health?

6. How does giving loving, centered attention to your work and your co-workers affect the health of your workplace?

Called into Healing, Chapter 3 (pp.59-80)

Science is only now beginning to explain what healers have described for centuries—that loving touch can heal. Smith cites Morton Kelsey's study of infants in orphanages who were not touched, and who entered into the condition called mirasmus where the children waste away and die.

> Babies need holding, touching, rocking, and soothing. Human touch is as necessary as food and water ... p.61

1. Have you ever known someone who was abused as a child? How did the lack of touch and loving affection, or the misuse of touch (hitting and shoving) affect them?

2. What precautions can you take to help someone who has been the victim of misused touch? See page 62 of *Called into Healing* for some suggestions. Our touch can be a determining factor in the outcome of healing.

3. Even when our hands are not in contact with someone's body, "the whole person" is touched during healing work (p.62). How would you describe "whole person" healing?

Smith describes the many scientists who have devoted themselves to understanding what scientific basis energy healing might have (pp.62-69, 71-75).

4. How necessary is it for you to have scientific support for the experiences you've felt when giving or receiving healing touch?

5. How do you describe how or why healing touch works when people ask you?

6. Smith says that healing is not a transference of the healer's own energy but the healer acts as a vessel or conduit for Higher Energy (God). How do you know when it is God's energy and not your own?

A pioneer of using touch to heal within the nursing profession is Dr. Dolores Krieger. After she observed the healing work of Oscar Estebany, (a natural healer) she wanted to harness the power she saw in his laying-on-of-hands for use within the medical field. She turned to Eastern science as she tried to understand how and why Therapeutic Touch is effective (pp.75-76). When describing the work of Oscar Estebany who attributed his healing power to Jesus, Smith writes:

> Her {Krieger's} rationale and explanation of the laying-on of hands had to be in words the scientific community could accept. Krieger believed that the ability to heal was an expression of a deep inner desire by the individual to help or heal another—to be of service … In the end she concluded that healing flows from compassion and is an expression of love at the highest level … This is not scientific language. It is "heart" language … p.77

7. When did you first become aware of your deep inner desire to help heal others?

8. Has your heart been opened or changed by doing healing work?

9. Why do you think compassion heals?

> Through presence, listening and touch, nurses are reawakening to the art of nursing. Healing is occurring not only for the patient, but for the nurse as well … p.80

10. Do you envision a similar reawakening and healing for the church as healing ministries become more common?

11. When you open to being a vessel or instrument of healing for others, God's love and grace flows through you for the good of another. Are you not then healed into wholeness as you reach out to help others?

Healing Others:
Emotional Release Work for Another

The fact that Jesus was willing to touch the "untouchables" in his culture meant that he not only healed them—he also accepted them. In our culture today, people with mental illness are often avoided, if not shunned. Even though most people don't know anything about how emotions are carried in the human energy field, they intuitively know that being around depressed people is draining. Being around grieving people makes us sad. Being around anxious people can trip our own anxiety, and being around hostile people makes us crabby. Being around schizophrenic or psychotic people makes us feel frustrated, and perhaps even unhinged ourselves.

Because of their effect on us, people with disordered thought patterns or emotions are often shunned, even within the church. **This is why it is so very important for us to touch them.** They usually feel completely alone in the world, and sometimes they really are.

The technique of emotional release can heal longstanding emotional problems. As Jesus enters the person's thoughts and memories, there is tremendous potential for healing. This is not to say that the origin of emotional illness is caused by their memories (although sometimes it can be). Mental illness is often rooted in biology. But the memories of those suffering from mental illness can become invaded by negative energy after the fact, with the onset of illness. In addition, their emotional instability will usually cause people to behave in ways that create lasting ill-will with others, and painful memories. In HTSM 103 Student Notebook, Smith writes:

> The memory does not go away, but the energy around the memory is changed. This is REAL.

It is one way that we can touch the untouchables today.

Emotional Release Work for Another[4]

This exercise is based on the work of Agnes Sanford and Linda Smith. When a client or friend recognizes troubling emotions are holding them back in life and they request inner healing from the work that you do, it is important you be strong and confident as the practitioner. Spiritual healing takes many forms. Often it is simply a matter of being enabled to give up our anxiety or worry in order to trust that God is at work in our lives.

- Begin with your own preparation through prayer, meditation and fasting to strengthen yourself for this kind of healing.

- Do a general energy assessment, asking the client if they see a physician regularly or if they are in counseling. Now, sit at the head of the table or at the side and place your hand on the client's heart. Tell the person you will be resting your hand there for some time. Agnes Sanford begins by asking the client if they had a happy childhood. Many longstanding emotional patterns actually began in childhood. If the answer is yes, then she asks, "When did you first recognize you were unhappy." Usually a memory will pop up. This may or may not be the original wound. The client does not have to disclose the memory that is troubling but it is helpful if they can identify the emotion they are feeling when they go to that memory. You can ask, "what are you feeling as you remember the scene."

- Be patient, this is the client's process and it may take time. You are to be a compassionate listener, not a solver of problems. The events in the memory are not important, the feelings are. Then, invite Jesus—or another symbol of God—to enter the memory. When it's a painful childhood memory, have the person visualize Jesus coming to them to protect them from those who are

---

4. Linda Smith, *Healing Touch Spiritual Ministry 103 Student Notebook*, *"Using Your Hands to Heal,"* 3rd edition, Arvada, Colorado: HTSM Press, 2010, pp.59-60.

hurting or abusing them. This usually brings deep healing for the sufferer. What does Jesus say or do?

- Encourage the client to feel what they were feeling in the memory, not just think about it. As they feel it, ask them to release it through the palm of your hand. If you feel heat in your palm, they are releasing the feeling. If you feel tingling, generally they are thinking about the feeling and not actually feeling it.

- The best way to support someone in this process is to watch and pray. Pray aloud that the Lord heal this broken place and remove this feeling from their heart and from their body.

- When you feel the heat in your hand start to diminish, pray that the Lord fill up their heart with positive loving energy—whatever is missing in their life. This might be love, worthiness, joy, clarity, patience, wisdom, abundance, compassion, etc. Then pray that God's love fill all the empty places in their heart. Finally, thank God for what has happened in this person's life.

- Tears will sometimes flow and they are not tears of grief but of joy at the release. Some people may experience a trembling throughout their body as they release the emotion.

- The memory does not go away, but the energy around the memory is changed. This is REAL.

Healing Ourselves: Meditation on the Healing Hands of Christ[5]

Let those hands that touched others so freely touch you. This is a peaceful and healing meditation … a guided visualization on the Healing Hands of Christ. It is suitable for your personal reflection time or it can be read slowly for group meditation.

---

5. Linda Smith, *Healing Touch Spiritual Ministry 104 Student Notebook* , *"Forming a Healing Practice,"* Arvada, Colorado, HTSM Press, 2010, pp. 69-70. Inspiration for this meditation comes from Thomas Droege, "The Healing Presence," pp. 134-137.

"Now he was teaching in one of the synagogues on the Sabbath. And just then there appeared a woman with a spirit that had crippled her for eighteen years. She was bent over and was quite unable to stand up straight. When Jesus saw her, he called her over and said, 'Woman, you are set free from your ailment.' When he laid his hands on her, immediately she stood up straight and began praising God." Luke 13: 10-13

- Gently closing your eyes let any distracting thoughts that come into your mind float by as if carried away by the wind. Pay attention only to the natural rhythm of your breathing as you relax in the peace and quiet of this place. Feel the movement of God's Spirit within you and around you. *(pause)*

- In your mind's eye imagine that you are with Jesus in a quiet, peaceful place, just the two of you. This can be a familiar place or some place that you create now in your imagination. Just notice the beauty of the surroundings, the peace which fills your heart, for you are in the presence of Jesus. *(pause)*

- Let all the stress you carry fade as you now open your heart to spending a few moments with Jesus the Healer. *(pause)*

- Focus your attention just on the hands of Jesus, those healing hands that he used so often to touch those whom he healed. What do those hands look like? Are they strong and rugged, like the hands of a carpenter? Or, are they smooth and soft, like the hands of a priest? Are they like the hands of a parent, stony and sure? *(pause)*

- There are no right or wrong ways to imagine the hands of Jesus. *(pause)*

- The hands of Jesus are healing hands. Call to mind the story of the woman in the gospel who was bent over with a debilitating back ailment. For 18 years she had had a back so severely bent that she always had to look at the ground. Imagine yourself in such a position. Now imagine Jesus putting his hands on your back as you are bent over. Feel the warmth of his touch and the gradual relaxation of your muscles. Gradually you straighten your back until you can look at Jesus and his healing hands. *(pause)*

- Scan your body right away now for any places that hold pain or discomfort or perhaps hold illness. Listen very carefully to what your body tells you about that. *(pause)*

- Symptoms are messages that our body sends us even when we aren't paying attention. Take a moment and listen. What is your body trying to tell you? *(pause)*

- Now imagine Jesus placing his hands at that place in your body that holds discomfort. Notice that the discomfort immediately begins to shift. Let the healing energy from his hands penetrate deeply into the muscles and other tissues of your body that are in need of healing. Take a moment to let this experience deepen. *(pause)*

- Slowly now, come away from your experience of the healing hands of Jesus by opening your eyes and returning to the presence of your surroundings. Take some time to quietly journal about your healing experience. *(pause)*

SESSION 4

The Connection between Faith and Salvation

Luke 8: 40-56
Called into Healing, chapter 4

Gathering

After everyone has arrived, read out loud the story of the generations of rabbis who prayed for their people to be saved (Smith, *Called into Healing*, pp.152-153).

One way to describe faith is "the need for help, the courage to ask God for help, and the hope that God will help us in the best way." It was the faith of the rabbis (not their knowledge) that God responded to when God saved the people. Discuss as a group: Have you known many people who have such faith? How could you tell? Do you feel that you have faith?

Healing Word

The pastor of a small church with a Healing Touch Spiritual Ministry held a healing service. One of those who came to the service was a little girl. She and her mother were living with her grandparents because three days ago the girl's alcoholic step-father had threatened to murder them (unfortunately, this is a true story). In the two days prior to the healing service, they had remained hidden in a safe house. To say the girl was emotionally fragile is an understatement. Yet, when the pastor called those who were at the service to come up for the laying-on-of-hands and prayer, she bravely went. The child had the faith to walk up the aisle alone … and as can happen during the laying on of hands, she was healed of things she no longer needs to remember.

31

Faith … what is it? Where does it come from? How does it save us, and from what? Why doesn't everyone have it all of the time? We have more questions than answers … and scripture provides us with examples rather than explanations. The accounts of Jairus and the woman healed from hemorrhaging are both examples of healing, saving faith.

A Girl Restored to Life and a Woman Healed

"Now when Jesus returned, the crowd welcomed him, for they were all waiting for him. Just then there came a man named Jairus, a leader of the synagogue. He fell at Jesus' feet and begged him to come to his house, for he had an only daughter, about twelve years old, who was dying.

As he went, the crowds pressed in on him. Now there was a woman who had been suffering from hemorrhages for twelve years; and though she had spent all she had on physicians, no one could cure her. She came up behind him and touched the fringe of his clothes, and immediately her hemorrhage stopped. Then Jesus asked, 'Who touched me?' When all denied it, Peter said, 'Master, the crowds surround you and press in on you.' But Jesus said, 'Someone touched me; for I noticed that power had gone out from me.' When the woman saw that she could not remain hidden, she came trembling; and falling down before him, she declared in the presence of all the people why she had touched him, and how she had been immediately healed. He said to her, 'Daughter, your faith has made you well; go in peace.'

While he was still speaking, someone came from the leader's house to say, 'Your daughter is dead; do not trouble the teacher any longer.' When Jesus heard this, he replied, 'Do not fear. Only believe, and she will be saved.' When he came to the house, he did not allow anyone to enter with him, except Peter, John, and James, and the child's father and mother. They were all weeping and wailing for her; but he said, 'Do not weep; for she is not dead but sleeping.' And they laughed at him, knowing that she was dead. But he took her by the hand and called out, 'Child, get up!' Her spirit returned, and she got up at once. Then he directed them to give her something to eat. Her parents were astounded; but he ordered them to tell no one what had happened." Luke 8: 40-56

The young girl and the grown woman had almost nothing in common. Jairus' daughter had all of the advantages that wealth and status could confer. The hemorrhaging woman, on the other hand, had no money—she had spent it all on doctors, who hadn't been able to help her. She was bleeding, which meant she was unclean. She was not allowed to touch anyone else, or she would make them unclean. She wasn't even allowed to touch the things that other people touched. The two of them were so different, but they had this in common: they needed help. Such a need for help … such a belief that Christ can help … such courage to reach out for help … these make up the substance of faith.

The Greek word usually translated into English as salvation is "sozo." Sozo is a word which has many meanings. In Mark 6:56 all who were sick were sozo'd, or healed. When someone was possessed by a demon, sozo described exorcism (Luke 8:36). In the case of Jairus' daughter, sozo is the word used to describe the girl's resurrection (Luke 8:50). When Zaccheus the tax collector, who had been stealing from people for years, gave away half of his wealth to the poor, Jesus said that sozo had come to his house, for the Son of Man had come to seek and to sozo that which is lost (Luke 19:10). When people were sozo'd, their relationship with God was restored, and those things that were most wrong in their lives were made right. Physical healing was often a factor of salvation, but it was part of a larger, more holistic picture. When ten lepers were cleansed/ cured, it was the one who returned to thank Jesus whom Jesus pronounced as sozo'd (Luke 17:19). Jesus himself used the word "sozo" to summarize his mission in John 3:17. "God did not send his son into the world in order to condemn the world, but that through him the world might be <u>saved</u>."

Both the hemorrhaging woman and Jairus' daughter were saved. The woman believed that one hidden touch would save her … and it did. Jairus believed Jesus when Jesus told him not to be afraid, and he brought Jesus home to save his little girl despite the laughter of the crowd … and Jesus did save her.

Faith is not the belief that God will do what we want how and when we want it done. Neither Jairus nor the bleeding woman received exactly what they wanted (she wanted an unobtrusive healing, and Jairus wanted a bedside visit for his daughter, not a resurrection). Neither got what they had in mind … but both were saved. Faith knows that Jesus can save us from whatever it is that we need saving from. It is the courage to ask for help, and the willingness to be open to what God brings into our lives.

Questions for Discussion

1. The hemorrhaging woman was trembling with fear when Jesus asked her to identify herself. Have you ever known people who have experienced healing, but have been afraid to tell others? Why do you think they were afraid?

2. Why do you think Jesus needed to make such a public display of her healing?

3. Jesus told Jairus "Do not fear. Only believe, and she will be saved." In what do you think he was asking Jairus to believe?

4. Jairus wanted Jesus to hurry up and heal his daughter, but Jesus was delayed by a "daughter" of his own. Have you ever encountered important people who believe that they're more entitled to healing than those who are less wealthy, and perhaps more vulnerable?

Called into Healing, chapter 4 (pp.81-98)

Many of our modern-day faith healers would have us think that if we only have enough faith, God will heal us, and if we are not healed, it is because we lack sufficient faith ... p.82

1. Have you known people who have held this opinion? What can we say to them?

2. More than any other factor, the unethical behavior of some so-called "faith healers" has damaged the credibility of healing ministries within the modern church. What can we do to provide a different understanding of what a healing ministry really is?

When we are facilitating healing for others, our belief in a good outcome, whatever that may be, does affect the healing work and bears our further investigation ... (p.82)

3. What is the difference between hoping for a good outcome, and demanding the outcome we believe is best?

4. Do you believe it shows more or less faith when we persist in hoping for a specific outcome?

One's faith, then, is not necessarily a prerequisite for receiving healing, but when it is present, it can add to the outcome ... p.83

5. If infants and comatose patients can benefit from the healer's healing prayers and healing hands, whose faith is it in a good outcome?

Herbert Benson found that "when our beliefs are added to the relaxation response, the effect is even more dramatic, quieting worries and fears." He came to call the combination of remembered wellness and the relaxation response, the "faith factor." The three components are: Belief and expectancy on the part of the patient, belief and expectancy on the part of the caregiver, belief and expectancies generated by a relationship between the patient and the caregiver.

6. How do you see the role of belief and expectancy fitting together?

7. How does "relaxation" fit into your belief system about healing?

8. When you move into prayer for someone's benefit, do your heart rate and respirations change as you connect into Spirit?

On pp. 84-85, Smith refers to the story of the man who brought his son to the disciples while Jesus was on the Mount of Transfiguration (Mark 9: 17-29). His son had seizures, and the disciples could not help him. When Jesus arrived he asked him if he could heal his son. "All things are possible for those who believe." "Lord, I believe—help my unbelief." Smith writes,

> And then we see Jesus reaching out and surrounding this man with the power of his Spirit, imparting to him the kind of faith that comes from the depth of prayer and forgiveness. It is this kind of healing that he taught his disciples so that they would continue his ministry when he could no longer be with them. It is this kind of healing that comes from a place of deep prayer and connection with God."
>
> "Our faith must be more than mere words—more than understanding with our minds. It must be felt at the heart, at the core of our spirit. Faith is soul work ... p.85

9. If healing work is heart work—how do you know when it is there and when it is not?

10. How do you keep your ego out of healing work? Do you ever struggle to believe?

11. What spiritual disciplines enable you to be deeply connected with God?

12. How do you know when in fact you are deeply connected "vibrationally," that is, are at one with God when you are doing this healing work?

13. On page 88, Smith discusses negative thought patterns. What negative thought patterns have held you, or others you know, back?

The power of prayer has been documented by many, including Dr. Larry Dossey. It is therefore of concern that prayer might be used to curse or hex others (pp.94-97). Smith describes the pitfalls of focusing on what is wrong with the person who needs healing, or in any way judging them, instead of directing loving intention for healing their way.

14. Can you think of a situation in which praying for a specific outcome, although it's well-intentioned, might be damaging?

15. Do you believe that our ambivalent feelings for someone else might interfere with our praying for healing for them? Smith advises that if we do find ourselves in a situation where we are asked to pray for someone toward whom we have mixed feelings, we first pray for ourselves, asking that our ambivalence and negativity be replaced by compassion and love (p.95).

In the closing pages of chapter 4, Smith speculates about the potential power of negative energy, negative thought forms, and negative prayers. Even when this energy isn't directed toward someone personally, it can be imparted to them through contact with the angry or negative person.

16. Have you ever observed or experienced the kind of dark energy that Smith describes the nurse imparting to her when he came in to start an IV?

17. What can you do to shield yourself from the negative energy or thoughts of others?

Healing Others: the Sign of the Cross Blessing[6]

The Sign of the Cross Blessing is a uniquely Christian technique. Smith writes,

> The brow, throat (lips) and heart energy centers are touched in this gesture, opening these centers to God's blessing and healing presence ... p.50

Blessing another is an act of faith. When we bless someone, we wish them well absolutely. We impart to them God's love and grace. Blessing is the opposite of cursing or hexing.

Using the Sign of the Cross Blessing may be a good way to protect someone who is under attack by the negative thought patterns, or by some other dark energy. The blessing remains in their energy field long after the treatment is over, and can protect them. If you want, as you do the Sign of the Cross Blessing, you can imagine sealing Christ light into their energy body.

- Begin by standing on the right side of the person who is to receive. Center and connect to the Holy Spirit. Set your intention for the work.

- Starting at the crown of the head, pass your right hand slowly and gently down through the center of the body. Your hand will pass over all the centers from the crown to beyond the root. You may want to hold your left palm up and open in a gesture of receiving light.

- Next, pass your right hand horizontally from the recipient's right to left over the brow center.

- Again, pass your hand vertically down through the center of the body, passing over all the centers.

- Next, pass your hand horizontally from right to left over the throat center.

---

6. Linda Smith, *Healing Touch Spiritual Ministry 103 Student Notebook, Using Your Hands to Heal*, 3rd edition, Arvada, Colorado, HTSM Press, pp.50-53.

- Pass your hand vertically down through the center of the body, passing over all the centers.

- Now, pass your hand horizontally from right to left over the heart center.

- Pass your hand vertically down through the center of the body, passing over all the centers.

- Repeat this series of gestures for as many rounds as necessary. Generally this technique is done for about 10 to 15 minutes or until the person is in a state of relaxation. You may end this technique by placing one hand on the recipient's heart and one hand on their brow.

There can be many variations of this Sign of the Cross Blessing. Allow the Spirit to guide you in your prayer as you gently bless the person before you. You may even want to pray affirmations with each horizontal and vertical passes over the energy centers.

Healing Ourselves

A beautiful prayer of faith is credited to St. Theresa of Lisieux:

> *May today there be peace within. May you trust God that you are exactly where you are meant to be. May you not forget the infinite possibilities that are born of faith. May you use those gifts that you have received, and pass on the love that has been given to you. May you be content knowing you are a child of God. Let this presence settle into your bones, and allow your soul the freedom to sing, Dance, praise and love. It is there for each and every one of us.*

At its root, faith is our soul's reaching out to God, trusting that we will meet love there. Faith trusts that not only are there "infinite possibilities"—but that the one who makes all things possible cares about us infinitely.

Called and Sent Out to Prepare the Way

Luke 10: 1-11, 17-20
Called into Healing, chapter 5

Gathering

After everyone has arrived, ask the group "Why do you give healing touch to others?" Their answers will probably be varied, but most people will say that they are drawn to Healing Touch or Healing Touch Spiritual Ministry because it is rewarding, they feel that it helps people and it brings them and others closer to God. It's far more than a hobby. It's a calling from God, a ministry.

Take a few minutes to explore what a calling is and what it means to be called to the ministry of healing touch. Fredrick Buechner wrote, "*The place God calls you to is the place where your deep gladness and the world's deep hunger meet*" (Frederick Buechner, *Wishful Thinking: A Seeker's ABC*, San Francisco: Harper San Francisco, 1993, page 119). Ask the group to reflect on that statement. How does giving healing touch give us deep gladness? What is the deep hunger of the world that is fed through our healing touch spiritual ministry?

Healing Word

Jesus was well into his ministry when he sent out seventy people on a mission. They were to travel in pairs, and to go ahead of him into the villages that he intended to enter. There, they were to eat with people, cure the sick, and proclaim that the Kingdom of Heaven had come near.

It's important to note that just a few short verses before the passage we're looking at here, in Luke 6:51-52, a village of Samaritans had refused to welcome Jesus when he came to them. His disciples James and John were angry with the villagers, and wanted to command fire to come down from heaven to consume them. Jesus rebuked his top disciples over this. That human tendency to be angry over slights, and to seek revenge, is contrary to Jesus' spirit. Jesus sent his followers to reach out to people, not to punish them. The role of the seventy was to prepare the way for Christ to visit people himself.

The Mission of the Seventy

"After this the Lord appointed seventy others and sent them on ahead of him in pairs to every town and place where he himself intended to go. He said to them, 'The harvest is plentiful, but the laborers are few; therefore ask the Lord of the harvest to send out laborers into his harvest. Go on your way. See, I am sending you out like lambs into the midst of wolves. Carry no purse, no bag, no sandals; and greet no one on the road. Whatever house you enter, first say, "Peace to this house!" And if anyone is there who shares in peace, your peace will rest on that person; but if not, it will return to you. Remain in the same house, eating and drinking whatever they provide, for the laborer deserves to be paid. Do not move about from house to house. Whenever you enter a town and its people welcome you, eat what is set before you; cure the sick who are there, and say to them, "The kingdom of God has come near to you." But whenever you enter a town and they do not welcome you, go out into its streets and say, "Even the dust of your town that clings to our feet, we wipe off in protest against you. Yet know this: the kingdom of God has come near." I tell you, on that day it will be more tolerable for Sodom than for that town …

The seventy returned with joy, saying, 'Lord, in your name even the demons submit to us!' He said to them, 'I watched Satan fall from heaven like a flash of lightning. See, I have given you authority to tread on snakes and scorpions, and over all the power of the enemy;

and nothing will hurt you. Nevertheless, do not rejoice at this, that the spirits submit to you, but rejoice that your names are written in heaven.'" Luke 10:1-12, 17-20

We have no idea who they were. What were their names? Some early manuscripts of Luke's gospel claim that there were seventy, others that there were seventy-two of them. How many of the towns they visited rejected them?

There is much that we do not know about these brave people who were called and sent out by Christ to proclaim the kingdom. What we do know is that when they were called, they answered. When they were sent, they went. And when they were welcomed, they brought into the kingdom many people who were open to Jesus' ministry. They shared the peace of Christ, they proclaimed the Kingdom of God, and they cured the sick. Sadly, not everyone wanted the Kingdom of God. When they were not welcomed, they wiped the dust off of their feet, and left.

For the most part, they seem to have been successful. After returning from their mission, they were filled with joy. They had been bathed in Christ's power—they had even performed exorcisms! Yet Jesus gently reminded them that it was not the authority that he had given them that mattered most. What most mattered was the love they had received from God. Being part of the Kingdom of God themselves was even greater cause for celebration than bringing the Kingdom to others.

Whoever the seventy were, they are our kindred spirits. Like them we rejoice when we are the conduit through which God heals others. We know that all Christians have their own, unique callings. While ours may be healing, others are called to make quilts or coffee, teach Sunday school, and to serve on church boards or councils. We are called and sent to heal. Others are called and sent to do other things. What matters more than what ministry we have been called to do is that we ourselves have been called by Christ to join the Kingdom. All of our names are written in heaven.

When the seventy returned from their mission, they spoke with excitement about those who had received their ministry—they didn't dwell on those who rejected them. Christ's ministry is far more comprehensive than Healing Touch or Healing touch Spiritual Ministry, and perhaps someone with a different calling from ours will be able to proclaim the kingdom to those who reject healing ministry in a way that they can welcome with peace and understand. But as for us, what a blessing it is to be called to our unique ministry of Healing Touch or Healing Touch Spiritual Ministry. What a gift it is!

For Discussion

1. Why do you think Jesus sent the seventy followers out in pairs, rather than alone or in larger groups?

2. Why did he tell them not to take money, clothes, or sandals, nor to greet anyone on the road?

3. How do you think they would have felt when they came to a community that did not receive them, and they had to "wipe the dust off their feet?"

4. Have you ever experienced "rejection" in the church for doing healing ministry? Did you shake the dust from your feet and move on?

5. Have you ever given or received the peace of Christ in the way Jesus describes?

Called into Healing, chapter 5 (pp.99-112)

Rather than specific techniques, it is likely that the seventy or so people Jesus sent out would have used the laying-on of hands in following his instructions to cure those who were sick. On pp.99-104, Smith writes

There are basically four steps in performing the simple form of the Laying-on of Hands:

Centering—connecting to God, your Source, though your heart center.

Intention—fixing your attention on God and on the flow—the movement of God's Spirit.

Assessment—taking in information through conversation, observation, and intuition, and allowing this information to enter at the heart level.

Treatment—acting as God's instrument and doing something—either hands on or off the body, still or moving.."

1. As you go through these steps, what role does intuition play for you when you give healing touch? Are you comfortable when you sense that your hands should move to a place not specified in the technique you're using?

2. Centering and intention are healing for the healer as well as necessary for healing others. So often when we give healing touch, we also receive. Take a moment to share with the group what you've received when you've given a healing touch.

When moving beyond the simple form of the laying-on of hands by allowing our hands to move through someone's energy field, we have stepped beyond what is recorded in the Scriptures. We just have no idea if Jesus and his disciples felt someone's pain and strove to brush it away. What may seem logical to us may not have been their experience. What is clear to us is that we have learned a great deal in the last 2,000 years about who we are as energy (spiritual) beings. We do not end at our skin but in fact, extend several feet out from the body. Just as pain can be found in the physical body, it exists as well in the energy body. Moving through someone's field to brush away the pain is therefore understandable.

3. As you practice this extended form of the laying-on of hands, can you feel the subtle differences in the field with your hands? How would you describe it? Does everyone's field feel the same or are they different? How do you interpret the meaning of these differences?

4. Smith says there are only two things you can do with your hands—move them or hold them still, and place them on the body or held above the body. How do you know when to do either?

Smith describes the young woman in a class she taught who burst into tears when her partner asked her "What would you like me to pray for?"

> I asked her if she was all right, and she told me that the thought of someone actually praying for her during healing work had never occurred to her. She was overwhelmed by the power of this spiritual work and acknowledged that she could not remember someone ever praying for her. (p.107)

5. Do you think the young woman's experience is common?

6. If so, how might the church respond?

On pages 109-111, Smith describes the healing ministry of anointing. She concludes,

> When anointing with oil is used in combination with the laying-on of hands, the effect can be quite profound.

7. Do you currently use oils in your healing ministry? What have you found effective?

8. What are your thoughts about this closing statement:

> So many ask why there are so few people attending church today. I wonder if it is because people, old and young, are not finding healing there. (p.112)

Healing Others: The Simple Laying-On of Hands

In Luke 10: 1-12, Jesus called and sent out seventy unnamed people. They were able to accomplish amazing things in their travels, and they were courageous enough to go out as he told them to—bringing no money, no spare clothes, trusting that God would provide for all of their needs. Still, what they accomplished was ultimately not their ministry—it was an extension of Jesus' ministry. They could not cast out demons, cure the sick, or proclaim the kingdom on their own power. The authority in which they acted was lent to them by Christ.

The simple laying-on of hands is the first technique we are taught in Healing Touch Spiritual Ministry. It may be easy to underestimate the power of this technique as we take the more advanced classes. Still, because it is not so much a technique as a prayer, the laying-on of hands draws our attention to the fact that while we may have advanced skills, all healing comes from God. Our ministry is an extension of Christ's. Because he is so powerful, Christ's will may be done in the simplest of interventions, as well as in the more complex ones. Amazing healing can come from the simple laying-on of hands.

The Simple Form of the Laying-On of Hands[7]

The simple form of the laying-on of hands can be performed anywhere. The person receiving can be sitting in a chair, standing at the altar rail, or laying on a bed or couch. There are basically 4 steps: centering, intention, assessment and treatment. Centering and intention are your interior preparation for doing the healing work, assessment is determining what to do (taking in information), and treatment is being open to the power of god flowing through your hands and your heart. It is your being a channel, conduit, or facilitator for the flow of divine energy. Simply put, there are only two things you can actually do with your hands—hold them still or move them, hold them above the body or on the body.

- Center yourself and invite the Holy spirit to fill you. Take a breath and breathe in God's love, sending it down through your body and out your feet to ground you on the earth. With the next

---

7. Linda Smith, *Healing Touch Spiritual Ministry 101 Student Notebook, Introduction to Healing Ministry*, HTSM Press, Arvada, pp.71-77.

breathe, bring it into your heart and expand it to fill up the space that surrounds you.

- Now set your intention for the highest good for this individual before you. Let go of your need for anything in particular to happen. Ask only to be a conduit or instrument of God's healing for this person.

- Ask the person where the problem is or what he/she would like you do do during this healing time. Listen from your heart.

- Observe their facial expressions, body language and positioning. Ask God for guidance in seeing the areas that need help.

- Now listen inside, where do you fell guided to place your hands—on the body or held above the body.

- Keep your awareness on the power of God. The goal is to help this flow of God's healing energy to move through the person before you.

- If words of prayer come to you while you are holding your hands on the person, just know that you can speak them in the silence of your heart or aloud as the Spirit directs. Just remember, this is not about proselytizing to your way of belief. It is about their healing.

- When you sense that enough is enough, slowly remove your hands and be in a place of gratitude for all that God as done.

Healing Ourselves:
Clearing Ourselves to Fulfill our Callings

Whenever Christians are called and sent into a ministry, it is a privilege and a blessing. The well-being of the minister will definitely affect their ministry. This is especially true with Healing Touch Spiritual Ministry. If we who have been called to Healing Touch Spiritual Ministry don't take care of ourselves, we won't be clear channels for Christ's healing love to pour through. Blockages within us can keep us from fulfilling our callings to heal. They can prevent us from heeding Christ's call to go where we are sent. It is not selfishness to monitor and to meet our own needs. It's common sense.

Pages 65-67 from the HTSM 101 workbook contain some helpful suggestions for those times when we may feel blocked. It may help to discern why we're blocked, how to redeem blockages and distractions, and what can be done to overcome our blockages. We are called and sent to minister, but remember Jesus' words to the seventy: "Rejoice because YOUR names are written in heaven." Be gentle with yourself. Christ's ministry is as much to us as through us.

- Spend quality time in prayer
- Learn to forgive others
- Listen to guidance
- Spend time alone to calm the inner chatter
- Simplify your life
- Be in service of others

Healing Churches

Luke 13: 10-17
Called into Healing, chapter 6

Gathering

After everyone arrives, ask them to describe the church in which they grew up, as well as the church they currently attend. What did they appreciate about their churches? What about their present church? How do they see God working through their church community? Why do they think most of the people who attend their churches come?

As a thought experiment, ask them to imagine how their congregations would respond if Jesus came to visit their congregation next Sunday? Are strangers welcomed in your place of worship?

Healing Word

The gospels make clear that, while the Romans carried out Jesus' crucifixion, it was the Jewish religious leaders who orchestrated the events leading up to it. One of the primary reasons they felt that Jesus' death was necessary was that he persisted in breaking the Law of Moses by healing people on the Sabbath.

The Sabbath … Today, when the stores are open 24/7, when sports tournaments are scheduled on Sunday mornings because that's when people will come, and when the notion of unplugging from the internet for even one day is unimaginable for many, the ferocity with which the Jewish leaders fought Jesus when he healed people on the Sabbath strikes us as almost ridiculous. Didn't they know that God wants people to be healed? Why shouldn't Jesus heal on the Sabbath?

Understanding the sacrifices the Jewish people had made in order to keep the Law of Moses sheds some light on the emotions involved.

Second Maccabees 7: 1-5 describes the horrific torture of seven brothers, who died while their mother watched. Why their torture and death? (They were fried alive!) They refused to eat pork. Why did they refuse to eat pork? They would rather die than break God's Law. Over one thousand Jewish men, women and children were massacred by the Greeks during the Macabbean revolt because they chose to die on the Sabbath rather than to break the Sabbath by fighting back against their attackers. When we contrast the willingness of religious Jews to die to keep the Law with Jesus' willingness to die in order to break the Law when he touched the sick and healed people on the Sabbath, it is inevitable that the Jewish religious leaders would become Jesus' enemies. Jesus clearly felt that God's work of healing was urgent, and that it was worth the price he would pay. For a fuller discussion of this, see Francis MacNutt's book *The Healing Reawakening*, pp.48-52.

Simply reading the gospels leaves us with a sense of the urgency of Jesus' healing ministry. Jesus would allow nothing to get in the way of his healing ministry, not even the Law of Moses … not even the hatred of those who wanted to enforce the Law. When healing was so important to Jesus two thousand years ago, it seems puzzling that the modern church has so easily left healing ministry by the wayside.

Jesus Heals a Crippled Woman

"Now he was teaching in one of the synagogues on the Sabbath. And just then there appeared a woman with a spirit that had crippled her for eighteen years. She was bent over and was quite unable to stand up straight. When Jesus saw her, he called her over and said, 'Woman, you are set free from your ailment.' When he laid his hands on her, immediately she stood up straight and began praising God.

But the leader of the synagogue, indignant because Jesus had cured on the Sabbath, kept saying to the crowd, 'There are six days on which work ought to be done; come on those days and be cured, and not on the Sabbath day.' But the Lord answered him and said, 'You hypocrites! Does not each of you on the Sabbath untie his ox or his donkey from the manger, and lead it away to give it water? And ought not this woman, a daughter of Abraham whom Satan bound for eighteen long years, be set free from this bondage on the Sabbath day?'

When he said this, all his opponents were put to shame; and the entire crowd was rejoicing at all the wonderful things that he was doing." Luke 13: 10-17

Did you notice what had crippled the woman for 18 years? Luke describes it as a "spirit." A spirit had kept her in bondage ... and her spiritual leaders would have kept her in bondage for one more day, too, if they could have. But the Spirit of Christ insisted that she be released NOW. Could Satan have been working through the religious establishment to cripple God's Holy Spirit within religion as clearly as he was working through the woman's back to cripple her? The tool that Satan chose was hypocrisy.

Demanding that others live up to standards that we are not willing or able to live up to is hypocrisy. When he healed the woman on the Sabbath, Jesus did indeed break the Law, which stipulated that rest and worship were the only activities permitted on the Sabbath. Healing was work. Jesus was guilty. His defense was not that he was innocent. It was that they, too, were guilty. It was inhumane not to care for animals on the Sabbath ... and it was likewise inhumane to let one of God's children linger under the Spirit of Satan that crippled her. The truth of his argument was so obvious that his opponents were put to shame.

The Spirit that cripples religious institutions might rear its head in your church from time to time. But it cannot stand up to the Spirit of Christ. The fact that demonstrating compassion for others was a hallmark of Jesus' ministry, and is a hallmark of any healthy church, will sway open minded people to support your healing ministry. Still, some will see your healing touch as breaking unspoken (and usually unexamined) rules. "We've never done that here before so we shouldn't start now" is one common unwritten church rule. As is "we don't want to rock the boat so we shouldn't ever do anything people might not like or understand." There's also the common (although frequently denied!) attitude in some churches that "this church exists to meet the needs of its members." Believe it or not, one church declared that "there will be no healing in this church!"

The title of this session is "Healing Churches." It has a deliberate double meaning. Creating Healing Touch Spiritual Ministries can be challenging work. Designing the nuts and bolts of your program may only come after you have been able to work for healing within your own congregation. What, if any, are the unspoken rules that "bind" your church, as the woman was bound by Satan? How can your congregation become a healthy community able to bless the healing ministry that the Spirit will work through you to create?

Questions For Discussion

1. What message would he have conveyed if Jesus had waited to heal the woman until the following day? What message did he send when he refused to wait even one more day to heal her?

2. Are there unspoken rules in your church that may hamper your healing ministry? What are they? How can your team work to heal and address them?

3. Luke's gospel tells us that when Jesus pointed out the hypocrisy of his opponents, they were filled with shame. Is shame ever healing or helpful?

4. If you have begun a healing ministry in your congregation already, how has it been received?

Called into Healing, Chapter 6 (pp.113-128)

As I have visited and participated in the worship services of many Christian churches ... Often, the one ministry I am most passionate about—healing ministry—is missing..." (p.113)

1. How many churches in your area have some sort of a healing ministry? What does that ministry involve?

Smith's vision is a ministry that will

> ...bring a healing touch to all those who need healing in body, mind, soul or spirit (p.114).

2. Who are the people who need healing in your church community?

Smith raises these questions on page 114:

- What would a healing ministry look like in your parish or in your congregational setting?
- Where do you start?
- Who can you talk to about your call to healing ministry?
- Is there an existing ministry in your church that a healing ministry could fit into?

Other questions Smith raises are:

3. How will you help your church leadership learn more about healing ministry?

4. What can you do to gain further pastoral support for your ministry?

5. How will you introduce healing ministry to your congregation?

In pp.116-120, Smith brings up some issues that need to be considered at the outset of planning a healing ministry, such as confidentiality, boundary or gender issues associated with healing touch, and consent forms. She lifts up the importance of pastoral supervision, as well as the value of working in pairs. On p.120, she has this to say about fear:

> I would like to think that as we do this work, we are coming from a heartfelt place, a compassionate, loving place for our fellow man and woman. But there may be those who interpret our efforts

differently and judge our actions as offensive or harmful, when that is not our intent. Some churches today may be fearful of having a healing ministry for these very reasons. Fear can stop the flow of grace. Fear can stop the actions of the Holy Spirit and keep us fragmented and closed to the presence of God.

6. Why might some people be afraid of Healing Touch? Is it fear of the unknown? Fear that it might be "New Age?" Fear that you might be healing through the power of Satan? (Honestly, since when is Satan interested in your health and well-being!)

7. Fear of the unknown does strange things. Could people actually be afraid of success and how this might change their safe and secure church life?

8. With all the attention the past few years about inappropriate touch happening in churches or by priests and ministers, is there a fear that the church is opening up to liability by having a healing ministry involving "touch?"

Developing a healing ministry involves preparing the congregation, training and commissioning healing ministry team members, developing policies and procedures, and closely supervising all aspects of the ministry. The scope of the ministry may involve healing and anointing services, or it may not. On pp.125-128, Smith lists churches that have begun healing ministries.

9. Which of the churches Smith describes is most demographically like yours?

10. Is there a healing ministry that you know of (it may or may not be listed in *Called into Healing*) that you'd like to use as a model for your healing ministry in your own congregation?

Healing Others

In the *Suggested Guidelines and Policies for a Healing Ministry* (2010), Smith writes about all of the concerns that ministers and lay people have raised in starting healing ministries. This is a compilation of suggested policies and guidelines for addressing concerns that may come up. Take time to go through this little booklet—which issues fit your situation? How would you adapt this work for your healing ministry?

Healing Ourselves

In her book *An Altar in the World,* Barbara Brown Taylor writes about the spiritual discipline of keeping the Sabbath. She calls it "the practice of saying no" (p.121).

That is a good way to talk about what the Sabbath really is. The good is the enemy of the best … so in order to say "yes" to God, we have to say "no" to other good things in life. "No, I won't be able work today because I'm going to church." "No, I can't help you, I have a prior commitment to my family." "No, I can't be the chair of that committee because I am committed to another one, and I want to do it well." We all have many competing demands on our time, and we must learn to say no to some of them in order to make room for the most important ones.

It might be helpful to take some time to journal. To what have you had to say "no" in order to pursue your healing ministry? To what might you need to say no in order to receive deeper healing for yourself? What are your true priorities, the things for which you really want to make the time? What can you say "no" to that will make more room in your life for God?

Going Home to Heal

Luke 8: 26-39

Called into Healing, chapter 7

Gathering

The connection between healing and exorcism is a mysterious one. One certified HTSM practitioner described to her class an experience that she believes was an exorcism. The woman who was on the table receiving healing claimed to be, and spoke as if, she was possessed by a demon. The healer prayed and surrounded her with Christ light. The darkness which had enveloped the woman began to recede. At some point, it simply wasn't there anymore. Just as turning on a light banishes darkness, so Christ light banishes dark energy.

Discuss as a group: have you ever felt yourself to be in the presence of negative, or dark, energy? How did you handle it? What can you do to protect yourself?

Healing Word

The deliverance of the Gerasene demoniac was a dramatic exorcism. The Gerasenes were not Jewish (which explains why there was a herd of pigs on the hillside.) The demons within the possessed man recognized Jesus, addressing him as "Son of the Most High God." They begged Jesus for mercy. They pleaded not to be sent "back into the abyss." So he sent them instead into a herd of pigs grazing on the hillside. As they had tormented the Gerasene demoniac, causing him to run away from his friends and family and to hurt himself with stones, they tormented the pigs, causing them to self-destruct by rushing pell-mell down the hillside to drown in the lake below.

The heart-rending aspect of this account is the response of the

Gerasenes to the man's exorcism. Rather than being happy that the demoniac was clothed and in his right mind, rather than thanking Jesus for what he had done for the man, they were terribly frightened by Jesus' demonstration of power over evil. Fear possessed the Gerasenes just as strongly as the demons had once possessed the naked, howling man who broke his shackles so that he could bruise himself with stones (Mark 5:5.)

Jesus Heals the Gerasene Demoniac

"Then they arrived at the country of the Gerasenes, which is opposite Galilee. As he stepped out on land, a man of the city who had demons met him. For a long time he had worn no clothes, and he did not live in a house but in the tombs. When he saw Jesus, he fell down before him and shouted at the top of his voice, 'What have you to do with me, Jesus, Son of the Most High God? I beg you, do not torment me'— for Jesus had commanded the unclean spirit to come out of the man. (For many times it had seized him; he was kept under guard and bound with chains and shackles, but he would break the bonds and be driven by the demon into the wilds.) Jesus then asked him, 'What is your name?' He said, 'Legion'; for many demons had entered him. They begged him not to order them to go back into the abyss.

Now there on the hillside a large herd of swine was feeding; and the demons begged Jesus to let them enter these. So he gave them permission. Then the demons came out of the man and entered the swine, and the herd rushed down the steep bank into the lake and was drowned.

When the swineherds saw what had happened, they ran off and told it in the city and in the country. Then people came out to see what had happened, and when they came to Jesus, they found the man from whom the demons had gone sitting at the feet of Jesus, clothed and in his right mind. And they were afraid. Those who had seen it told them how the one who had been possessed by demons had been healed. Then all the people of the surrounding country of the Gerasenes asked Jesus to leave them; for they were seized with great fear. So he got into the boat and returned.

The man from whom the demons had gone begged that he might be with him; but Jesus sent him away, saying, 'Return to your home, and declare how much God has done for you.' So he went away, proclaiming throughout the city how much Jesus had done for him." Luke 8:26-39

Why do you think that Jesus answered the demon's request to enter into the herd of swine who were feeding on the hillside? One common explanation is that Jesus wanted to prove, beyond the shadow of a doubt, that the demons were gone from the man they had once possessed. The carcasses of the swine, bobbing up and down in the lake, would have served as vivid proof that the demons had been cast out of the man and had entered the pigs.

Despite this proof in pig flesh that the demons had been exorcised, despite the fact that they could see that the man who had been naked and crazy was sitting at Jesus' feet clothed and rational, there was no gratitude from the Gerasenes. They apparently preferred the presence of a demoniac whom they could shackle or banish to the presence of a man who had the supernatural power to exorcise demons. Perhaps the man's possession and resulting behavior had completely dehumanized him in their eyes. Whatever their reasoning, the Gerasenes did not gladly welcome the demoniac home and thank Jesus for returning him. In terror, they begged Jesus to leave.

With friends like that … who can blame the demoniac for wanting to go with Jesus?

But Jesus would not let him leave his home. This man who had been cleansed from darkness by the light of Christ was commanded to go back to his community and shine Christ's light there. He was to tell the Gerasenes, who were so frightened of Jesus, about the healing from darkness he had received. And he was to tell them about Jesus the healer.

Following Jesus' healing path is never an escape from reality. It is an invitation into the deepest truth that there is: the power of God's love for all people, especially those who disappoint and devalue us. This is the way of the cross. Jesus loved those Gerasenes who asked him to leave, but they were so frightened of him that they would never listen to what he said. So he sent the man whose life he had saved home. Clothed and in his right mind, this man would no longer break shackles, bruise himself with stones or cause fear. He would walk through the city proclaiming what God had done for him. He would point other to the Great Physician by telling the truth.

Like the Gerasene demoniac, we are not healed for the purpose of escaping from our communities or our problems. The gift of health has been given to us so that we can go home, tell everyone what God has done for us, and point them to Christ.

Questions for Discussion

1. For whom do you feel more sorry—the Gerasene Demoniac or his people, who were so afraid that they asked Jesus to leave their community? Why?

2. In your life, when have you been the most afraid? What made you afraid? Remembering your fear, can you sympathize with the Gerasenes?

3. Do you think it was cruel for Jesus to refuse the man's request to leave with him?

4. The man who had been healed of possession told everyone what Jesus had done for him. In Mark's gospel we're told that "everyone was amazed" by what he said (Mark 5:20.) This kind of response to a testimony of healing is only possible when we believe the person who is testifying. What has been your experience with Healing Touch? Have you ever told anyone what Jesus has done for you?

Called into Healing, chapter 7 (pp.129-150)

In the opening pages of chapter 7, Smith describes two people she met briefly who changed her perspective on life forever. She writes,

> ...they had both learned the art of spiritual presence. The light shone through them, and I was changed. These 'teachers' held simple jobs, ones that would not have appealed to me. However, they elevated their work through their simple presence...

> "The spiritual presence that we bring into our relationships flows from our connectedness with the Divine. It can bring healing to all kinds of situations—to our families, peers, work situations, churches, communities, towns and cities ... For me it is the first step in learning how to be an instrument of healing for others ... p.130

1. Have you met people who have learned the art of spiritual presence? Why do you think that such people bring healing wherever they go?

2. The art of spiritual presence comes from being connected to the divine while simultaneously being connected to the specific place in which we live, and to the specific people with whom we come into contact. Describe a time when you have experienced this sense of connection to both God and other people. Are such times rare in your life? If so, why?

Using Maggie McKivergin's framework, Smith describes three different levels of healing presence: physical, psychological and therapeutic. These levels of presence are integrated when we are practicing the art of spiritual presence. Smith writes:

> Being truly in the moment, connected to our Source, to God, we cannot help but extend compassionate caring in our touch and in our word. In essence, we radiate wholeness and beauty. This is not an easy task, but it becomes easier with practice...

> In true Christ consciousness, all outcomes are blessed ... p.132

3. What kinds of things can we do to bring ourselves "into the moment" so that we can be truly present for others?

4. When you give healing touch, do you believe that all outcomes are blessed? Why or why not?

5. Moving beyond the act of giving healing touch, do you believe that all of the outcomes of your efforts in your home, your workplace, and your church blessed? If not, how would your life change if you accepted on faith that they were? Might such acceptance help you to become a healing presence in those environments?

6. As this Bible Study is being written, the people of Haiti are rebuilding their country after a devastating earthquake which killed and/or injured hundreds of thousands of people. Can someone be "healthy" in an environment such as that? Explain your reasoning.

> If we feel moved to be an instrument of healing but have not yet learned that we must be spiritually connected to God in our hearts, our efforts will show few results. Healing comes from the heart, where God's love and compassion reside. When we are connected to this divine energy, infinitely more is possible. This is one of the essential differences between Christian healing and secular healing ... p.136

Healing Touch is used in traditional nursing settings and in churches. No matter whether the environment in which it is given is religious or secular, Healing Touch seems to bridge the secular and the spiritual aspects of human existence. Ironically, both the medical and the religious communities sometimes seem at times to be uncomfortable with this intersection.

7. How can our understanding of healing be expanded (balanced) to honor contributions from both the secular and the spiritual communities?

8. Does it seem to you that the medical and religious communities have different "turf?" Why or why not?

On p. 139, Smith describes the importance of our own self healing. She writes:

> Self healing needs to take place on all levels: physical, emotional, mental and spiritual. What are you doing to bring your whole being into balance? Just as all healing is heart work, healing ourselves is also heart work. We must be kind and gentle with ourselves … p.139

9. Do you find it easier to understand healing as a gift you can help God give to others, or as a gift that God wants to give to you? Explain your answer.

10. Can we heal others without first experiencing healing ourselves?

11. In what practices do you engage in order to promote your own self healing? Who helps you in your path of personal healing?

In the last section of chapter 7, Smith writes about the healing presence of Christ.

> When Jesus told his followers to be compassionate as God is compassionate, he was referring to the Jewish tradition that views God as Mother, as birther. To say that God is compassionate is to say that God is 'like a womb.' Compassion was more than just a virtue for Jesus; it was a vehicle for social action…

> We pay a price in healing work. We may run the risk of having our offer of healing hands rebuffed, ridiculed or even rejected. We may be attacked verbally or even physically. Our jobs may be on the line, or our relationships may be in jeopardy if we persist in expressing our healing ways … p.148

As followers of Christ, we are aware that Jesus' perfect wholeness radiated from his complete abandonment to his Father's will. He was without the rebellion of sin, and accepted all that he was given as from his Father's hand. Living out his faith in God and his holy trust in the compassion of his Father was the fulfillment of the Kingdom of God in human life. We are given a glimpse of this kingdom; we are invited to join this way of life, throughout our lives as Christians.

12. How does our understanding of the compassion of God move us to help others?

13. Jesus constantly said "the Kingdom of God is at hand." To what extent is it "in our hands?"

14. Have you paid a price for your healing work? If so, why have you chosen to pay the price rather than giving up?

15. The Gerasene demoniac was sent back to his own people to proclaim the healing Jesus offers. Do you find it easier, or harder, to be a healing presence for those who know you best? Can you explain why?

Healing Others

We began this chapter talking about exorcism and possession by demons. In the biblical world view and indeed, the world view of most peoples of that era, physical illnesses were thought to be caused in some way by malevolent or evil spirits. If we understand that evil spirits are of a "low vibration" and the angels carry a "higher vibration or energy," then calling upon the archangels to assist you in removing unwanted energy or energies of a "low vibration" you could assist someone in relieving unexplained headaches, vague pains in the body, or agitation which are unrelated to any particular physical cause. In this healing technique, we call upon the archangels Gabriel, Uriel, Raphael and Michael who guide the four dimensions of a person's energy system—etheric, emotional, mental and spiritual—to help clear the energy field. We call this technique "Casting an Angelic Net."[8]

---

8. Linda Smith, *Healing Touch Spiritual Ministry 105 Student Notebook*, 3rd edition, *The Art of Listening to Spiritual Guidance*, Arvada, Colorado: HTSM Press, 2010, p.69.

As always, center and call upon your spiritual guidance before beginning this healing work. It is important that call upon the Christ Light to fill you. Have the person who is to receive, lay face up on a massage table or bed.

- After you have assessed the field for symmetry and balance, go and stand at the head of the table with your hands held above the field. Call upon the archangel Gabriel as you cast a red net around the body/field and off the feet by moving your hands in a wide circle, closing the circle under the table. Then draw the net off the body/field catching any darkness or low vibration and sending it to the light by casting it out the door or window.

- Next, go to the right side of the table and call upon the archangel Uriel as you cast a green net (moving your hands in a similar arching circle around the body/field and closing it under the table). Then draw the net off the body/field in a similar way, casting it to the open doorway or out a window.

- Now go to the left side of the table and call upon the archangel Raphael and use a mustard colored net around the body/field, connecting your hands under the table as before. Again, cast the net out the door or window.

- Now standing at the foot of the table, call upon the great archangel Michael and cast a golden net around the entire body/field and draw it off in a similar manner. Send it to the light.

- You will want to check in with the person and find out how they feel. Check the energy field for symmetry and balance. If you still sense that there is "darkness" or low energy stuck in the field, then repeat this praying silently for the health and well-being of this person. Call upon additional help of the saints—those who have gone before us and who now stand at the throne of God.

I have found that this can be a powerful healing technique especially when performed with the assistance of others who hold the space in prayer.

Healing Ourselves

> When we tap into the Christ presence, we transcend our own
> limited selves, producing an energy of caring. Caring does not
> always mean doing something; it may simply be about be-ing
> present. And in the be-ing, the Christ Light is able to flow out and
> fill the space around us … p.149

16. In what unhealthy spaces, and/or with what unhealthy people,
    do you find yourself daily right now?

17. Which of those spaces and people needs most to be filled with
    Christ Light?

18. Has anyone ever told you that you "radiate?" What do you
    think the observer is really seeing in you?

In your mind's eye, imagine that space, and those people, bathed in
Christ Light. The bitter face of an enemy becomes soft in Christ's love
… the angry look of a child who thinks you're a tyrant when you set
loving boundaries becomes accepting … the hostile face of someone
who hates you becomes understanding.

Remember that there is no moment except for the present
moment. This vision, in your mind's eye now, is how you really see
those people in your life for as long as you can hold this vision in your
mind's eye.

Sadly, people can and do resist healing. Even as we flood others
with Christ Light, we remember the words of St. John. The true light,
which enlightens all people, has come into the world. But people
choose darkness rather than light because their deeds are evil. People
can and do hold onto the darkness of their choosing, but we Christian
healers choose to hold onto the light of Christ. When we hold others in
loving intention, we bathe them in Christ's light as well.

We end this session with another meditation which is a group
exercise in distance healing.

On Surrounding Others with Healing Light[9]

Jesus said, "Where two or three are gathered in my name, I am in their midst." He taught his disciples to pray for others and we know that the early Church was known for its powerful healing ways. We today can gather in God's name and pray for one another. This exercise is both a prayerful and energetic one and is done when several people can join together to send healing light to those in need.

- Begin with all those assembled standing in a circle holding hands. Centering together, breathe God's light and love into your hearts, filling up your whole being.

- Now, send this light down your legs and out the soles of your feet into the earth as if you have roots. Connected above and below, feel the strength of God's grace within you. You are now filled with golden light.

- Bring your awareness now to your heart and with intention, send some of this light down your right arm and out your palm to the person on your right.

- Receive this light from around the circle through your left palm and send it out again around the circle so that there is a continuous circle of light connecting all your hearts. Let this circling light continue, speeding it up so that it becomes one band of brilliant healing light. Feel God's love and compassion fill your whole being.

- Now with intention, send beams of light from your hearts into the center of the circle. Bring into consciousness all those for whom you would like to pray. See their faces in your mind's eye. See their brokenness and need for healing.

---

9. Linda Smith, *Healing Touch Spiritual Ministry 103 Student Notebook, Using Your Hands to Heal*, 3rd edition. Arvada, Colorado, HTSM Press, pgs.78-79.

- Now send the healing light from the center of the circle to all the corners of the earth to surround those individuals in need of your prayers and healing. See the faces of each person you are sending healing light to surrounded with this glowing healing light.

- See their brokenness mended as they receive God's healing grace in this moment. Visualize them whole and in balance. Picture each person as you silently (or verbally) name those to whom you are sending healing energy. Stay in focused attention as much as possible.

- Within your heart now, move into a place of gratitude for the gift of this healing energy. Continue to be in a place of love and compassion as you offer thanks for the healing that has taken place.

- Visualize the light returning back now to the center of the circle, and back into your own hearts. Gradually slow the stream of energy that is circling and call it home back through your left palm and back into your own heart.

- Take a breath and know that where two or three are gathered in God's name, there can be healing. And know that you can send this prayer of healing at any time.

Healing: Both Destination and Journey

Luke 18: 18-26

Called into Healing, chapters 8

Gathering

In the 1940's a psychiatrist named Rene Spitz performed a well-known study in a small South American orphanage. He compared the development of a group of children raised in this orphanage to a group of children raised by their incarcerated mothers in prison. Spitz observed and recorded what happened to ninety-seven children who were in the orphanage. The nurses changed their diapers, fed and bathed the children, but they did not hold, cuddle, or talk to them. After three months of receiving only minimal care for their bodily needs many of the children showed signs of abnormality. They did not eat or sleep well, and they lay in bed with a vacant expression in their eyes. After five months, they lay whimpering, with troubled and twisted faces. Often, when a doctor or nurse would pick up an infant, it would scream in terror.

Almost one third of the children died during their first year in the orphanage, but not from lack of food or health care. They died of a lack of touch and emotional nurture. Seven more died the second year. Only twenty-one of the original ninety-seven survived, most suffering serious psychological damage. The children who were raised by their mothers in prison, by contrast, all survived.

This study demonstrates something that we intuitively know to be true. Love is a basic human need. We need a soft voice to comfort us, a kiss, a gentle pat on the shoulder just as we need food, water, clothing and shelter. Love is intangible, yet essential. We cannot be healthy without it.

In chapter 8 of *Called into Healing* Smith writes about the mystery at the heart of healing touch work: the union of love between God, the practitioner, and the person who is seeking healing. The power of love, so intangible and yet so crucial to human health and development, is difficult to quantify in a medical setting.

Discuss as a group: why and how does loving touch heal us?

Healing Word

A central theme in Jesus' teaching was the nature of the Kingdom of God. He told parables about God's Kingdom to eager listeners. He demonstrated the reality of God's Kingdom by forgiving sins, by healing people, and by embracing people whom his religious peers rejected. He promised his listeners that they could be children of God, and he also challenged them to be like God in their dealings with others. God, Jesus reminded them, *"is kind to the ungrateful and the wicked. Be merciful as your Father is merciful"* (Luke 6:35-36). God's Kingdom is rooted in the love of God for God's children. Our participation in the Kingdom of God is rooted in our sharing of the love of God with others.

The Commandment to Love

"But I say to you that listen, Love your enemies, do good to those who hate you, bless those who curse you, pray for those who abuse you. If anyone strikes you on the cheek, offer the other also; and from anyone who takes away your coat do not withhold even your shirt. Give to everyone who begs from you; and if anyone takes away your goods, do not ask for them again.

Do to others as you would have them do to you.

If you love those who love you, what credit is that to you? For even sinners love those who love them. If you do good to those who do good to you, what credit is that to you? For even sinners do the same. If you lend to those from whom you hope to receive, what credit is that to you? Even sinners lend to sinners, to receive as much again. But love your enemies, do good, and lend, expecting nothing in return. Your reward will be great, and you will be children of the Most High; for he is kind to the ungrateful and the wicked." Luke 18: 18-26

When someone does something to hurt us or someone we care about, the emotions that we experience might be hatred, disappointment and/or sadness. These emotions are natural responses to difficult situations, and we cannot control them. Jesus never said that we were not supposed to experience emotions, even negative and damaging ones. What he did say is that we are not to act on these feelings. We are not to judge one another, but we are to let God do the judging. Jesus taught that we are to love everyone, even our enemies (especially our enemies!).

When people treat us kindly, we find it easy to feel affection and gratitude toward them. We can call this feeling "love." But loving people for whom we naturally feel affection, such as our family members and close friends, is not much of an accomplishment. Anyone can do that, and most people do. The love that Jesus calls us to is not a love based on emotion, but one based on a decision. Essentially—to be a child of God, to choose the Kingdom of God, is to choose to love people for whom we naturally experience aversion, even hatred and anger. It is a decision to be completely free from our own judgment of others, no matter how justified our judgment may be.

There is no sign that points to the Kingdom of God more brightly than the love Christ bids us have for one another. This love is to be the hallmark of the church. In John's gospel, Jesus told his followers that their love would be a sign to the world that they were followers of Christ (John 13:35). The Christian way is forgiveness that frees both the transgressor and the victim from the judgments of the past. The Christian way is the refusal to judge others, which allows them and us to experience new life. The Christian way is best described as our union with God which leads to our decision to treat with love those toward whom we feel negative emotions.

This power of love, as intangible yet as crucial as the air we breathe is the essence of the Kingdom of God.

Questions for Discussion

1. Is there anyone in your life whom you would consider your enemy? Explain your answer.

2. Who do you find easy to love? Why is it easy to love them?

3. When do you feel like it's challenging to love other people?

4. Is it a struggle for you not to judge other people? Why or why not?

5. Do you often judge yourself?

6. In what kinds of practices can we engage our hearts to be more loving and accepting?

Called into Healing, chapter 8 (pp.151-165)

Healing touch bridges the gap between our spiritual or energetic reality and our physical being. In healing touch, medical science and theology merge. Whether we speak in terms of universal energy or God, for those who are pointed toward God the experience of giving and receiving healing touch is an experience of the vast and infinite love of God which we experience during prayer. Smith writes,

> Over time, my paradigm around health care, healing, and the role of prayer began cracking—everything that had given meaning and purpose to my life was giving way to a new understanding of prayer, healing, and my role in it..p.152.

1. A paradigm is a framework through which we make sense of the reality we experience. Paradigms are the rock-bottom assump-

tions that we make about how things work. Has your experience of Healing Touch or Healing Touch Spiritual Ministry cracked (or changed) the paradigm through which you view God?

2. Has Healing Touch or Healing Touch Spiritual Ministry cracked (or changed) the paradigm through which you view human health?

The heart is the center of our being. I'm referring not to the physical heart or some emotion that we may identify as coming from the heart but rather the 'heart center,' where we connect to our deepest ground, to Spirit … p. 152

3. How do our heart centers, our connection to our deepest ground, to Spirit, help us to understand Jesus' teaching that we are to love one another?

4. Is it possible to command someone to love someone else? Explain your answer.

On pages 153-154, Smith speaks of the transformation that accompanies being used as an instrument, conduit or courier of God's divine grace. She writes of a new way of life, a new way of being, that will accompany (and also serve as the catalyst for) our healing journey. Our intentions are purest when they come from a desire to be at one with God's will.

When your intention becomes one with God's intention, everything is possible, including healing. So how do you know when your intention is joined with God's intention? By sensing it inside. It is an inner knowing that comes through the process of discernment … p.154

5. What are some barriers that you might experience as you set your intention for God's will to be done?

6. Have you ever given healing touch to someone, and felt that "nothing good" was accomplished? What might be the reasons for those feelings?

7. How do you know when your heart's intention matches God's intention?

Smith writes of the "me" that wants to see specific results, and that knows what is the "best" outcome for a healing touch treatment.

> This 'me' thinks it is spiritual and an instrument of God's healing. This 'me' is not so outrageous as to be strange to onlookers … For example, when good results are happening in our healing work with others, it takes undue delight in what it has accomplished. Many of the great Christian mystics have talked about this 'false self' and ways to recognize and control it, but it will always be with us. You cannot destroy the shadow side, but it can be redeemed, transformed, and eventually integrated into one's being … p.154

8. What are the signs of the presence of the false self in your life?

9. When you become aware that your ego is enjoying what God is doing through you when you are giving healing touch, what do you do?

10. Should the results of healing touch ever be evaluated? Please explain your answer.

11. Do you ever feel "drained" after giving healing touch to someone else? Whose energy did you give away?

12. Did you get into this work thinking that this would be a great way to support yourself financially with service being second? If so, how has this influenced your work as a healing practitioner?

Throughout the rest of Chapter 8, Smith describes different spiritual practices that help us to dismantle the false self. Which of these practices do you use? Which have been most helpful for you?

• Emptying Mind and Heart to Make Space for Spirit

• Surrendering to Divine Direction

- Cultivating Inner Stillness
- Cleansing and Releasing Old Resentments and Pains
- Allowing "New Life" to Rise Out of our Ashes
- Listening to Wisdom
- Shielding—Filling One's Field with Light
- Centering—Connecting to Ground
- Placing One's Self in God's Hands, Asking to be a Vessel or Channel for Healing

Healing Others—The Sacred Heart Blessing[10]

(Ideally you will be seated at the head of a massage table but this healing technique can also be done with the recipient seated in the chair with you standing behind. This technique works very well when using an essential oil on your hands. You might want to consider frankincense, Joy, lavender, sandalwood, or other fragrant oil that is appropriate for the moment. Center and connect with the Spirit, setting your intention for the work.)

- Place your left hand on the recipient's heart center. Your left arm will extend down the side of the head.

- With your right hand, place your palm on the right side of the recipient's head. Your fingertips will extend down over the ears. Then gently move the head, pressing it against your left arm. You will be holding this position for 5-10 minutes.

- Now you are ready to begin this Sacred Heart Blessing. Focus your attention on your own heart center and with the aid of the Holy Spirit go to a place of unconditional love in your own heart for this person whom you are holding in your arms.

---

10. Linda Smith, *Healing Touch Spiritual Ministry 104 Student Notebook*, *"Forming a Healing Practice,"* Arvada, Colorado, HTSM Press, 2009, pp. 56-58.

- Connect with the Sacred Heart of Jesus, remembering the great love that he holds for each of us. Your prayer is one of blessing this person with wholeness, balance and harmony. See them receiving whatever healing they need in this moment. See their brokenness mended with the oil of gladness, the oil of joy.

- As you continue to hold your hands in this position, if it seems appropriate, you can pray aloud: "The living love of Jesus now fills you. This warm light fills calms and heals your heart and mind. Be at peace."

You may notice how the energy balances between the brain and the heart. Emotional releases may occur and there may be tears. Reassure the recipient and simply be a compassionate listening companion. This is not an opportunity to fix anyone or give advice. Simply be a healing presence as Christ would be.

Healing Ourselves: Examining One's Heart[11]

This exercise is best done at the end of the day when activities have wound down and the environment is quiet. Do not put any music on.

- Come into a quiet place within. Take a deep breath and let go of the cares of the day … feel your body begin to sink into your chair … notice if there are any places that hurt or are tense … breathe into these areas, letting go of all that is tight or sore…

- Ask God to shed light on the day's experiences … allowing each one to pass before your eyes … start with the events of your morning and move through the day … Be the observer and just notice all of the day's activities without judging or censoring…

---

11. Linda Smith, *Healing Touch Spiritual Ministry 105 Student Notebook,* "*The Art of Listening to Spiritual Guidance,*" Arvada, Colorado, HTSM Press, 2010), pp. 49.

- Thank God for being present in all of the day's happenings … Acknowledge the many ways that God has gifted you and cared for you this day…

- Go deeper now … taking several more deep breaths. Listen to God speaking to you through the day's experiences … Sift through your moods, feelings, urges…

- Notice how God has been at work within your life this day … These are the footprints of the Holy One…

- Acknowledge that God's love will always be greater than your weaknesses … Taste God's mercy for you…

- Resolve to respond to the Spirit with greater faith tomorrow.

Journal the thoughts and inspirations that came to you during your reflection.

SESSION 9

Transformative Healing

Luke 17: 11-19

Called into Healing, Chapter 9 and *Epilogue*

Gathering

In chapter 9 of *Called into Healing* Smith states that healing is:

> …more than a mastery of skills. Healing is a function of the heart. It is an incomprehensible mystery … The health-care system that I have been a part of rewards practitioners when they are able to meet outcome criteria and to discharge patients with no further treatment needed … p.168

Discuss the pros and cons of evaluating healing in terms of the medical outcome alone. Do you believe that contemporary health care providers can be trained to tap into the power of their hearts (to delve into the mystery of healing) or are they best left to focus on mastering traditional medical skills? Do you think someone can be cured without being healed? Likewise, can someone be healed without being cured?

Healing Word

In session 3, you learned about the strict regulations surrounding leprosy. The disease itself was difficult, but the social stigma and the emotional trauma resulting from social isolation would have been as cruel as the physical symptoms. Lepers needed physical, emotional, social and spiritual healing.

Nine of the lepers who approached Jesus in Luke 17 were cured of leprosy, but only one of them demonstrated gratitude. Jesus told the Samaritan leper who returned to thank him after he had been cured that his faith had made him well (or "sozo'd" him.) Faith perceives the presence of Christ even in illness. Faith transforms illness (whether it is cured or not) into gratitude.

Jesus Cleanses Ten Lepers

"On the way to Jerusalem Jesus was going through the region between Samaria and Galilee. As he entered a village, ten lepers approached him. Keeping their distance, they called out, saying, 'Jesus, Master, have mercy on us!' When he saw them, he said to them, 'Go and show yourselves to the priests.' And as they went, they were made clean.

Then one of them, when he saw that he was healed, turned back, praising God with a loud voice. He prostrated himself at Jesus' feet and thanked him. And he was a Samaritan. Then Jesus asked, 'Were not ten made clean? But the other nine, where are they? Was none of them found to return and give praise to God except this foreigner?' Then he said to him, 'Get up and go on your way; your faith has made you well.'" Luke 17: 11-19

I have watched many people prepare to die, but I'll never forget Irene. She was first diagnosed with cancer when she was a newlywed in her twenties. She bravely withstood chemotherapy, radiation, social isolation and multiple surgeries. When asked how she felt, no matter how sick she was, she would try to smile. The root of Irene's name means "peace" in Greek. She was well named.

Eventually, Irene knew that she would lose the life she had lived with so much love. After her funeral, I was surprised to receive a card from her, addressed to me in her own handwriting. It was a thank you card for the visits she and I had shared. A note in the card from Irene's mother stated that before she died, Irene had written over one hundred and fifty thank you cards to her friends, her family members, her neighbors, her doctors, her nurses and nursing aides. Her last words to me, after I prayed with her on the morning she died, were "thank you." She croaked the words out of lips dry and parched, because she was unable to eat or drink anything.

She died … and she died healed. I am convinced that it was the gratitude that she sincerely felt toward God for letting her wake up each morning alive that transformed her into one of the most whole (and holy) people I have ever known.

There is a distinction to be made between healing and curing. Curing restores someone who has a disease to the level of health and function that they were at before they became sick. Healing is what we call it when people are mentally (and sometimes physically) transformed. When people heal, they become more than they were before their illness began. Ten of the lepers were cured … they were restored to the state of health they had enjoyed before the onset of their disease. But only one of them was healed. Only one of them recognized that being cured was a sign pointing toward the divinity of Christ, who had cured him. His faith in Christ, his recognition that his cure came from Jesus, was the faith that healed him.

Like breath is a sign of life, our appreciation of our lives and the gratitude we demonstrate toward God and others is a sign of healing. Some people who have been cured from disease may feel a tremendous amount of anger toward God for allowing them to become sick in the first place. Others who are not cured know that Christ is with them, and they are filled with the peace that surpasses all human understanding even on their deathbeds. These are the people who have been healed. Their faith has saved/healed them.

Questions for Discussion

1. While ten of the lepers were made clean from leprosy, Jesus only describes the one who came back to express gratitude as being "made well" or "saved." How is gratitude "wellness," or "salvation?"

2. The leper who returned to thank Jesus was a Samaritan. Samaritans worshiped the same God as the Israelites, and they were racially related, but the relationships between Samaritans and Jews were constantly simmering with conflict and enmity.

This is why the fact that the person who returned to thank Jesus was a Samaritan is quite significant. Do you believe that healing and wellness diminish racial tensions and cultural conflict?

3. Can you describe a time when you have given thanks to God because you recognized God's hand in a situation whereas others took God's work in their lives for granted?

4. The thankful leper clearly understood that his healing had come from Jesus. Do you believe that all healing (whether thanks is given or not) is a gift from God? Explain your answer.

Called into Healing, chapter 9 and Epilogue, pp.167-188

In the opening pages of chapter 9, Smith addresses the perception that healing sometimes (at least on the surface level) seems to either succeed or to fail. When healing is evaluated solely on the basis of physical outcomes, the element of mystery is removed. She writes,

> Perhaps we have operated far too long from the premise that if it is broken we can surely fix it. But we are not machines—we are embodiments of mystery...
>
> What is this mystery of healing? When our lives are out of balance, it seems as if our spirit and our body are not in harmonious communication ... Our bodies are intricately interwoven with our spirits. What affects the body affects the spirit, and what affects the spirit affects the body. This is mystery ... p.168

1. In your experience, what are the symptoms that someone's spirit and body are not in harmonious communication?

2. Why do you think that our spirits and our bodies are so mysteriously connected?

> Prayer that comes from the heart is a prayer of intimacy, love and tenderness. Our deeper and truer selves—the selves created by God—come forth out of the shadows when we pray from the heart

... (This is) the self that delights in the moment and the self that accepts its dark passions, the self that loves fully, the self that is whole. This true self is always present and connected to God whispering in our hearts ... p.170

3. How aware of your true self are you in your daily life?

4. To "accept our dark passions" is difficult for many Christians. The true self Smith refers to is the product of both original sin and original grace. Why is understanding the shadow side of ourselves necessary for our own healing, and for the healing God can use our hands to give to others?

"Prayer is the natural response to awakening to the Spirit's call to ministry, be it healing, or any form of service. Awakenings can be many little subtle events that bring us to a deeper awareness of God's calling or they can be earth-shattering events like divorce, loss of relationships, loss of job, our own illness, or the death of a loved one. When awakenings happen, we no longer go on as usual ... p.171

5. Can you point to the spiritual awakenings in your own life?

6. Do you generally embrace awakenings, or do you reject them?

On pages 172-173, Smith describes the stages of prayer. The first stage is purgative prayer, in which we become less judgmental and less likely to engage in negative thinking. Purgative prayer helps us to see our need to change, and is characterized by our conversations with God. Purgative prayer heals, purifies and transforms us. The second stage of prayer is illumination, which Smith describes as contemplative surrender guided by love. This prayer lets us open ourselves to the guidance of God's Spirit through love, and it is characterized by the quieting of the mind in total surrender to Love. Illumination contains both consolation and desolation (the Dark Night of the Soul spoken of by St. John of the Cross). The third stage of prayer is union with God, or ecstasy. In this prayer we see God in all things, and all things in God.

7. What have been your experiences with these stages of prayer?

8. Can our prayers develop in a different order than purgative-illumination-union?

> I have already suggested many ways to bring us to that place of willingness on the path as we develop our healing skills. What else do we need to do to become an "Everyday Mystic" with a generous heart and a healing hand?
>
> ...Lectio Divina
>
> ...Centering Prayer
>
> ...Spiritual Companions and Mentors
>
> ...Do the Work of the Heart ... pp.176-183

9. Have you used these spiritual practices in your prayer life?

10. Do you consider yourself an "Everyday Mystic?"

11. What most helps you to stay centered in Christ in your everyday life?

12. Do you find it difficult to keep a rhythm in life?

In her Epilogue, Smith writes

> ...each person has the power to influence much larger circles of the human family. Many by their prayers hold the webbing of humankind together...

> I invite you to look within and examine your hearts. Ruah, the breath of God, is blowing upon us all ... As we heal ourselves, our inner light grows brighter, and we begin to be a sign of hope for all of those who need healing ... it is my hope that, with courage, we will recognize the healing abilities available to us through God for one another. What better place to start than with our very own church and spiritual communities where we strive to live the gospel mandate to teach, preach and heal ... p.188

13. How has Healing Touch or Healing Touch Spiritual Ministry affected your faith life?

14. In what ways do you feel called to bring a healing touch ministry into your church?

15. You have a healing story to tell. How can you tell your story to others within your faith community?

Healing Others—Blessing of the Senses[12]

For more than a thousand years it was a practice to bless the physical body by anointing the senses, hands, and feet as an anointing for healing the sick. This was actually a very holistic approach which through time was lost. It became anointing at one's final moments upon this earth. Only in the past 40 or so years as this anointing begun to change. This technique is based on that ancient tradition and can be performed with the recipient either reclining, or sitting in a chair.

If you will be using anointing oil with this healing technique, you may want to consider frankincense or myrrh, two of the oldest Bible oils used by the church for holy anointing. Frankincense was used for spiritual awareness and to promote meditation and uplift the person's spirits; myrrh was used for instilling deep tranquility and inner stillness. Or, consider using spikenard for profound sense of peace, sandalwood for tranquil effects on troubled souls, balsam for clarity of mind and spirit or cedarwood to help release nervous tension and stress related to survival.

- To begin this healing technique, first center and connect with Spirit, setting your intention.

- Now, put a few drops of your chosen anointing oil in the palm of your hand then gently rotate both your palms together in a clock-wise fashion.

---

12. Linda Smith, *Healing Touch Spiritual Ministry 102 Student Notebook, "Introduction to Judeo-Christian Anointing,"* Arvada, Colorado, HTSM Press, 2010, pp.49-51.

- Place one hand on the brow and the other hand behind the head. *"Bless this person with keen insights and clear thinking; with kindness and wisdom; with knowledge of who he/she is in the sight of God."*

- Next, place your palms over each ear and hold for several minutes. *"Bless this person with clear hearing and with ability to listen to the Voice of God and act accordingly in their life."*

- Now, place your palms gently over the eyes with the heel of your hand on the brow and the palms cupped over the eyes. (If the oil you have chosen is a strong one, raise your hands several inches so as not to irritate the eyes.) Hold this position for several minutes or until you feel the energy equalize in your palms. "Bless this person with good eyesight and inner vision to see more clearly the path that is theirs."

- Now, place one palm cupped over the throat and the other palm directly behind the neck and balance the energy at the throat, front and back. *"Bless this person with an ability to speak their truth in love and to make their needs known. Bless them with an enthusiasm for life, with joy and an ability to laugh. Bless with an ability to breathe in the breath of God and to breathe out what needs to be let go."*

- Now take the recipient's hand, holding it between both of your hands to open the palm energy center. *"Bless this person with hands that touch all of life with gratitude and reverence."*

- Now take the recipient's other hand and do the same blessing.

- Now, go to the feet and hold the recipient's foot with one hand above and one hand on the sole of foot. Wait until the energy balances. *"Bless this person's feet that walk upon the earth. May God bless them with a firm foundation, grounded and centered in life."*

- Go to the other foot and repeat the same gesture.

• Now go to the heart and place both hands on the heart, finishing your prayer of blessing. *"Bless this person with a healthy heart and a compassionate, loving heart, filled with generosity and kindness."*

Healing Ourselves-Finding a Rhythm in Life

Healing, whether we speak of personal healing or healing for others, is about harmony and balance in one's life … Janet Mentgen (said) "We cannot be a spark of light for someone else if our spark has gone out..

Mentgen gives us some guidelines that have worked for her in finding a rhythm in life. First, there is physical clearing, taking care of the body … Second, there is emotional clearing, expressing our hurts and our pains, which is a necessary part of life … Third, there is mental clearing, where we change our cognitive thought processes and patterns … Fourth, she identifies the use of sacred space (sacred space creates within us both inner and outer harmony) … Fifth is the principle of silence (speaking only when necessary to conserve energy) … Sixth is holy leisure, which brings balance into our lives and restores us from our workload … Seventh is holy relationship, which is about commitment, faithfulness and honoring those relationships in our lives … pp.184-185

Take some time to journal about how you clear your body, emotions, and mind. Can you form some sacred space? Is there any way you can incorporate holy silence, holy leisure, and holy relationships into your days? Following Janet Mentgen's suggestions will look different for everyone. What is the rhythm in your life?

Some Concluding Thoughts from Tammy and Linda— Being a Healing Presence for Others

Whether we are born into our faith or we choose it, for Christians healing is part of our namesake. Healing is not just something God does through us when we pray with others, lay hands on them and anoint them. Those are valuable practices, but they are only the tip of the iceberg. The more we are called into healing, the more we realize that healing is not what we do so much as it is who we are. We bear the Light of Christ into our homes, our communities, our churches and our work settings. Our path as Christ's followers is to be a healing presence. Our path is one of radical forgiveness, and complete acceptance of all that our Father brings into our lives.

We hope that whether you have used this guide in a group or for your own personal reflection, it has accomplished its purpose to nourish your faith and to strengthen your calling to healing ministry. Luke gives us many insights into the healing ministry of Jesus— insights which inspired Linda to write her first book *Called into Healing*. Where you will go with this material will be determined by your prayers, reflections and meditations about your own call to healing. We hope that this study is more than thought provoking—that it leads you to conviction and to action. We are sadly aware that some Christians who have felt called to heal have had their ministries rebuffed or even rejected. Forgive those who do not understand, shake the dust off your feet, and continue to travel on the path Christ has called you to journey. It is a path of love and joy that you do not walk alone.

The Healing Touch Spiritual Ministry Program

Healing Touch Spiritual Ministry is a program that teaches healing ministry from a Judeo Christian perspective to Christians of all denominations. For those needing a certification in this educational process, it is available through the Institute of Spiritual Healing and Aromatherapy which sponsors the Healing Touch Spiritual Ministry program. Based in the scriptures, this education integrates prayer, hands-on healing and anointing with healing oils. For the convenience of the students, the curriculum is divided into basic and advanced. The Basic program consists of 5 courses which cover the history of healing in Christianity, the roles of prayer in healing, various healing techniques derived from the laying-on of hands found in the scriptures and anointing with therapeutic or medicinal essential oils, many of which were used in the time of Jesus. The healing techniques bring balance and harmony to our being—physical, emotional, mental and spiritual. Often, pain is relieved, emotions released, spiritual comfort is felt, and well-being is restored.

The advanced program has 2 courses six months to a year apart. Students are guided in developing a healing practice either for family and friends, in a private practice or a healing ministry within a church, or in developing a clinical focus to a practice within a hospital, hospice or other institutional setting.

Courses are taught throughout the United States and in some foreign countries as missionary outreaches. Continuing education is offered for both nurses and massage therapists.

Vision and Mission

The vision of the Healing Touch Spiritual Ministry Program is to help restore healing in Christianity and more importantly, in our world.

This is no small task and involves all of you as well. Our mission is to provide educational programming to enable students to integrate the spiritual and scriptural aspects of healing ministry, prayer, the laying-on of hands and anointing with essential oils in faith communities or in ministry/service settings.

Please see our website for more information at www.ISHAhealing.com and for a schedule of classes near you.

The New Testament Record of Healing

Healing by Touch Alone or with Words					
Healing	**Matthew**	**Mark**	**Luke**	**John**	**Acts**
Peter's mother-in-law	8:14	1:30	4:38		
Multitudes	8:16	1:32	4:40		
A leper	8:2	1:40	5:12		
Jairus' daughter		9:18	5:22	8:41	
Woman with issue of blood	9:20	5:25	8:43		
A few sick people	13:58	6:5			
Multitudes	14:34	6:55			
Deaf and dumb man		7:32			
Blind man (Gradual healing)		8:22			
Child with evil spirit	17:14	9:14	9:38		
Blind Bartimaeus	20:30	10:46	18:35		
Two blind men	9:27				
Woman bound by Satan			13:10		
Man with dropsy			14:1		
Malchus' ear			22:49		
Man born blind			9:1		
Beggar at the temple gate—Peter and John					3:6
Father of Publius with dysentery—Paul				14:8	
Paul's blindness—Ananias					9:17
Young man who fell from window—Paul					20:8

Healing by Word, Faith or Exorcism

Healing	Matthew	Mark	Luke	John	Acts
Man with unclean spirit		1:23			
Many demons		1:39			
Man sick of the palsy	9:2	2:3	5:17		
Man's withered hand	12:9	3:1	6:6		
Multitudes	12:15	3:10			
Gerasene demoniac	8:28	5:1	8:26		
Syrophoenician's daughter	15:22	7:24			
Centurion's servant	8:5		7:2		
Dumb demoniac	9:32				
Blind and dumb demoniac	12:22		11:14		
Multitudes	4:23		6:17		
Multitudes	9:35				
Multitudes	11:4		7:21		
Multitudes	14:14		9:11	6:2	
Great multitudes	15:30				
Great multitudes	19:2				
Blind and lame in temple	21:14				
Widow's son			7:11		
Mary Magdalene and others			8:2		
Ten lepers			17:11		
Multitudes			5:15		
Various persons			13:32		
Nobleman's son				4:46	
Impotent man				5:2	
Lazarus				11:1	
Cripple at Lystra—Paul					14:8
Aeneas paralyzed for eight years—Peter					9:32
Woman with a spirit of divination—Paul					16:16
Woman who died in Joppa—Peter					9:36

Large Group Healings
Recorded in the Acts of the Apostles

In addition to the individual healings by the Apostles and disciples, there are ten passages in Acts which refer to the healing of large numbers of people. They seem to refer to healing as a natural part of the Christian community.

Acts 2:43. "Awe came upon everyone, because many wonders and signs were being done by the apostles."

Acts 5:12. "Now many signs and wonders were done among the people through the apostles."

Acts 5:14-15. "Yet more than ever believers were added to the Lord, great numbers of both men and women, so that they even carried out the sick into the streets, and laid them on cots and mats, in order that Peter's shadow might fall on some of them as he came by."

Acts 6:8. "Stephen, full of grace and power, did great wonders and signs among the people."

Acts 8:6-8. "And the crowds with one accord listened eagerly to what was said by Philip, hearing and seeing the signs that he did, for unclean spirits, crying with loud shrieks, came out of many who were possessed; and many others who were paralyzed or lame were cured. So there was great joy in that city."

Acts 8:13. "Even Simon himself believed. After being baptized, he stayed constantly with Philip and was amazed when he saw the signs and great miracles that took place."

Acts 14:3. "So they [Paul and Barnabas] remained for a long time, speaking boldly for the Lord, who testified to the word of his grace by granting signs and wonders to be done through them."

Acts 15:12. "The whole assembly kept silence, and listened to Barnabas and Paul as they told of all the signs and wonders that God had done through them among the Gentiles."

Acts 19:11. "God did extraordinary miracles through Paul, so that when the handkerchiefs or aprons that had touched his skin were brought to the sick, their diseases left them and the evil spirits came out of them."

Acts 28:9. "After this happened,[the healing of the father of Publius] the rest of the people on the island who had diseases also came and were cured."

Translations are from the New Revised Standard Version of the Holy Bible